WOMEN IN HISTORY

Women of the Roaring Twenties

❧

Clarice Swisher

LUCENT BOOKS
An imprint of Thomson Gale, a part of The Thomson Corporation

THOMSON
✦
GALE

Detroit • New York • San Francisco • San Diego • New Haven, Conn. • Waterville, Maine • London • Munich

For Jim and Lee

LIBRARY OF CONGRESS CATALOGING-IN-PUBLICATION DATA

Swisher, Clarice, 1933–
    Women of the roaring twenties / by Clarice Swisher
        p. cm. — (Women in history)
    Includes bibliographical references and index.
    ISBN 1-59018-363-0 (hardcover : alk. paper)
    1. Women—United States—History—20th century—Juvenile literature. 2. Nineteen twenties—Juvenile literature. 3. Women—United States—Social conditions—History—20th century—Juvenile literature. 4. Women—United States—Economic conditions—History—20th century—Juvenile literature. 5. Women in popular culture—United States—History—20th century—Juvenile literature. I. Title. II. Series.
HQ1420.S93 2005
305.4'0973'0904—dc22
                                                                                    2004023410

Contents

Foreword

The story of the past as told in traditional historical writings all too often leaves the impression that if men are not the only actors in the narrative, they are assuredly the main characters. With a few notable exceptions, males were the political, military, and economic leaders in virtually every culture throughout recorded time. Since traditional historical scholarship focuses on the public arenas of government, foreign relations, and commerce, the actions and ideas of men—or at least of powerful men—are naturally at the center of conventional accounts of the past.

In the last several decades, however, many historians have abandoned their predecessors' emphasis on "great men" to explore the past "from the bottom up," a phenomenon that has had important consequences for the study of women's history. These social historians, as they are known, focus on the day-to-day experiences of the "silent majority"—those people typically omitted from conventional scholarship because they held relatively little political or economic sway within their societies. In the new social history, members of ethnic and racial minorities, factory workers, peasants, slaves, children, and

women are no longer relegated to the background but are placed at the very heart of the narrative.

Around the same time social historians began broadening their research to include women and other previously neglected elements of society, the feminist movement of the late 1960s and 1970s was also bringing unprecedented attention to the female heritage. Feminists hoped that by examining women's past experiences, contemporary women could better understand why and how gender-based expectations had developed in their societies, as well as how they might reshape inherited—and typically restrictive—economic, social, and political roles in the future.

Today, some four decades after the feminist and social history movements gave new impetus to the study of women's history, there is a rich and continually growing body of work on all aspects of women's lives in the past. The Lucent Books Women in History series draws upon this abundant and diverse literature to introduce students to women's experiences within a variety of past cultures and time periods in terms of the distinct roles they filled. In their capacities as workers, activists, and artists, women exerted significant influence on important events whether they conformed to or broke from traditional roles. The Women in History titles depict extraordinary women who managed to attain positions of influence in their male-dominated societies, including such celebrated heroines as the feisty medieval queen Eleanor of Aquitaine, the brilliant propagandist of the American Revolution Mercy Otis Warren, and the courageous African American activist of the Civil War era Harriet Tubman. Included as well are the stories of the ordinary—and often overlooked—women of the past who also helped shape their societies myriad ways—moral, intellectual, and economic—without straying far from customary gender roles: the housewives and mothers, schoolteachers and church volunteers, midwives and nurses, and wartime camp followers.

In this series, readers will discover that many of these unsung women took more significant parts in the great political and social upheavals of their day than has often been recognized. In *Women of the American Revolution,* for example, students will learn how American housewives assumed a crucial role in helping the Patriots win the war against Britain. They accomplished this by planting and harvesting fields, producing and trading goods, and doing whatever else was necessary to maintain the family farm or business in the absence of their soldier husbands despite the heavy burden of housekeeping and child-care duties they already bore. By their self-sacrificing actions, competence, and ingenuity, these anonymous heroines not only kept their families alive, but kept the economy of their struggling young nation going as well during eight long years of war.

Each volume in this series contains generous commentary from the works of respected contemporary scholars, but the Women in History series particularly emphasizes quotations from primary sources such as diaries, letters, and journals whenever possible to allow the women of the past to speak for themselves. These firsthand accounts not only help students to better understand the dimensions of women's daily spheres— the work they did, the organizations they belonged to, the physical hardships they faced—but also how they viewed themselves and their actions in the light of their society's expectations for their sex.

The distinguished American historian Mary Beard once wrote that women have always been a "force in history." It is hoped that the books in this series will help students to better appreciate the vital yet often little-known ways in which women of the past have shaped their societies and cultures.

Introduction:
The New Woman

The 1920s were a challenging time for American women. As had always been the case, women were expected to raise children, keep house, provide emotional support for their husbands, and in myriad ways contribute to American society. During the 1920s, however, those demands came to seem less and less compatible. Particularly for middle-class women, roles evolved in ways that often left women feeling pulled in two or more directions at once. Historian Nancy Woloch notes: "Indisputably, the decade was a crucible of contemporary middle-class roles. It was also a crossroads at which different themes of women's history overlapped and intertwined."[1]

Sometimes, women of the 1920s responded to the competing demands by rebelling against authority. Expected to be serious paragons of propriety, for example, many chose instead to be frivolous and devote themselves to sensual pleasure. So at odds is the image projected by women of the 1920s with that of the past that social historians refer to the "New Woman" in discussing how these individuals lived and dealt with the challenges they faced.

Middle-class women had plenty of outlets for their energy. They could, as earlier generations had done, focus their time, energy, and resources on the common good, trying to improve the lot of all women. In the past women had worked together to gain for themselves the right to vote. Much more needed to be done, however. Women still lacked any real power to make decisions regarding childbearing, for example. And although woman's suffrage was now the law of the land, the right of black women—and men—to vote was widely ignored.

Nevertheless, many exciting and glamorous distractions offered themselves to the New Woman. She could attend to her appearance by poring over the latest clothing styles. She could spend evenings at parties and movies. She could follow the latest sensational stories about celebrities in the newspapers and movie magazines. Often, young women chose to be anything but serious.

Women who elected a more serious social role faced challenges of their own. In the past, most women had accepted the idea that their role was to feed, clothe, and nurture their families. The conservative element of society urged women to remain homemakers. If a woman chose a different path, she had to overcome doubts about her capacity to meet the intellectual demands of a profession. Even though women were attending college in large numbers, those who made decisions regarding hiring or admission to professional schools—usually men—dismissed women's career aspirations. Moreover, if a woman chose to marry and have a family, she could expect little help from her husband when it came to caring for the children or other domestic duties. The New Woman who chose to combine domesticity with a career had to experiment with new ways to manage her time and energy to meet the demands of being a wife, mother, and working woman.

Whether the New Woman chose domesticity, career, or some combination of the two, she faced yet another issue: how to respond to the materialism of 1920s society. In the twenties, growing prosperity combined with advancing technology to put hundreds of new products on the market. Mass-produced clothing and canned foods were widely available; labor-saving devices such as washing machines were affordable even for people of modest means. Advertisers bombarded women, who were the chief purchasers of products for the home, with entreaties to buy the latest inventions and innovations. Advertisers very cleverly used psychology to foster the impression that women were doing their jobs if they

In 1926 two women do the Charleston, a dance craze in the 1920s, on a rooftop ledge of a Chicago hotel.

Members of the League of Women Voters in Missouri organize a voter registration drive in 1925. With passage of the Nineteenth Amendment in 1920, women in the United States won the right to vote.

bought their products. Those who refused, the ads implied, should feel guilty for falling short of society's expectations. As a result of advertising, the items that women purchased could contribute to their image as homemakers and to the social status of the family. The fashion items, such as clothing and makeup, that women purchased were claimed to contribute to personal attractiveness and success with male partners. In this way, being a consumer became part of the New Woman's identity.

Substantial numbers of women took up the challenge of a career or job outside the home. Sometimes, women persevered to overcome barriers and gained admission to professions such as law and medicine. Others took up jobs, such as work in textile mills, that were readily offered to women. Whatever work they chose, however, women found themselves

Women of the Roaring Twenties

undervalued when it came to pay. Employers routinely paid women less than men for the same work.

Such inequity motivated still other women to continue the drive for reform that previous generations had taken up. Activists campaigned for an amendment to the Constitution that would specifically grant women equal rights. Others sought to organize women workers to achieve equity through the use of strikes.

As had always been true, poor women, both white and black, faced the greatest challenges. At the same time, they had the fewest options open for dealing with those challenges. As in the past, they had to work hard just to earn enough money to ensure survival for themselves and their families.

Even though the 1920s offered new employment opportunities in industries previously closed to women, often the women who took these jobs found themselves exploited. A poor woman could do little besides enduring the low pay and poor working conditions imposed on her. For the poor, being a New Woman meant new burdens, not opportunities.

No matter what her social standing, race, or level of education, the New Woman found the 1920s a time of uncertainty. Perhaps feminist Ethel Puffer Howes best summarized the situation when she said in 1929, "The last ten years have seen an extraordinary flux in the position, the activities, and most of all in the inner attitudes of women."[2]

Chapter 1:
The Defiant Spirit

During the decade of the 1920s, young women led the way in carving out a new place in American society not just for themselves but for their mothers and even their grandmothers. The attitude the young displayed was defiance, a tendency to rebel against the customs, traditions, and values followed by their elders. According to historian Dorothy Brown, by "challenging the old ways, [young] women stood at the center of the struggles of a culture at the crossroads."[3] Many young women defied widely observed norms of dress and behavior. These young rebels also refused to take life seriously and appeared not to value hard work. Instead, many young women concentrated on pleasing themselves. This defiant disregard for norms and traditions was symbolized in the young woman known as the flapper. Nancy Woloch comments on the significance of this image: "The flapper, with her aura of self-indulgence and independence, came to personify the 'point of view' of her generation."[4] Gradually, the flapper became the model for middle-class women across America.

Flapper Clothes and Hair

The revealing clothes that were the flapper's hallmark presented a particular challenge to these young women's elders. Women in previous decades had worn full skirts that covered their legs in keeping with the standards of modesty; flappers wore skirts that were tight and ended at the knee. Whereas their elders donned tight corsets that gave them the waistlines that fashion dictated, flappers wore the minimum of undergarments. Flappers also wore high-heeled pumps, exposing the upper part of their feet. As hemlines went up, necklines went down, sleeves were shortened as well, and some flappers even went sleeveless in the evening. To go with their knee-length skirts, flappers wore flesh-colored stockings—made of silk or rayon—which they rolled below the knee. The overall objective was to leave little to the observer's imagination.

Although such modes of dress shocked many adults, at least some parents encouraged their daughters to follow the new style. One mother said, "No girl can wear cotton stockings to high school. Even in winter my children wear silk stockings."[5] The flapper's style quickly became all the rage. One young woman who wanted to wear a short skirt but was concerned that her legs were unshapely asked a fashion consultant what to do. The consultant advised her, "There are so many legs to look at these days, maybe yours won't be noticed."[6]

Not only did they wear short skirts, but flappers wore their hair short. Such a style was in sharp contrast to the previously common practice of wearing hair long, tied up in a bun. For their haircuts, flappers went to barbershops despite warnings that barbershops, male refuges where foul language and crude jokes were the norm, were not places where proper young women should go. Writer Marvin Barrett quoted from a newspaper that editorialized that "the free and easy atmosphere often prevailing in barbershops is unsuitable to the high standards of American Womanhood." Barrett

The Flapper's Style

The flapper, confident, defiant, and independent, symbolized the decade of the 1920s. She set the style in clothes and hair and the standard in social behavior. G. Stanley Hall happened to meet a flapper one day coming in his direction. He recorded his impression of her in the June 1922 issue of the *Atlantic Monthly* magazine. His article is reprinted in *We, the American Women*, edited by Beth Millstein and Jeanne Bodin.

She wore a knitted hat, with hardly any brim, of a flame or bonfire hue; a henna scarf; two strings of Betty beads, of different colors, twisted together; an open short coat, with ample pockets; a skirt with vertical stripes so pleated that, at the waist, it seemed very dark, but the alternate stripes of white showed progressively downward, so that as she walked, it gave something of what physiological psychologists call a flicker effect. On her right wrist were several bangles; on her left, of course, a wrist watch. Her shoes were oxfords, with a low broad heel. Her stockings were woolen and of brilliant hue. . . . This was in January, 1922, as should be particularly noted because, by the time this [essay] meets the reader's eye, flapperdom, to be really *chic* and up-to-date, will be quite different in some of these details.

went on to dismiss such concerns: "What the American women want is a good short shingle [basic short haircut] and never mind the atmosphere."[7] By the late 1920s, nearly all young women were wearing short, or bobbed, hair, and large

Dressed in a revealing skirt, silk stockings, and high-heeled pumps, a flapper dances on the deck of a ship.

numbers of women in their thirties and forties had cut theirs as well. Even many women in their sixties had adopted the new fashion.

Perhaps even more at odds with prevailing norms than her clothing and hair was the flapper's use of makeup. Previously, makeup was considered to be something only prostitutes would use in any quantity. But now makeup became as commonly seen as short hair. Historian Frederick Lewis Allen reports, "Women who in 1920 would have thought the use of paint [makeup] immoral were soon applying it regularly as a matter of course and making no effort to disguise the fact."[8] The cosmetics industry boomed with sales of rouge and lipstick and expanded with the use of perfume, face powder, and mascara. By 1929, mainstream magazines aimed at women were promoting makeup. *Ladies' Home Journal*, for example, advertised lipstick prominently as a touch of scarlet with an alluring quality that lasted for hours.

New Attitudes Toward Sex

It was not just in their appearance that young women, particularly flappers, defied traditional practice. Whereas women of the late nineteenth century had been reluctant to talk about sex and even more reluctant to admit that they enjoyed it, young women now exhibited a new willingness to discuss sex. In part, the impetus for such openness came from the ideas of psychologist Sigmund Freud, whose writings about the harmful effects of repressing sexual feelings had become widely accepted. Doing so, Freud claimed, would cause neuroses, or mild forms of mental illness. The new attitude toward sex went beyond mere talk. Historians Beth Millstein and Jeanne Bodin note: "Sexual freedom was approved. Women openly challenged the 'double standard' of morality that said one way of behavior was acceptable for men but not for women."[9] Young women went to parties where they indulged in kissing and erotic touching—known as petting—with the young men who attended. During intermissions at dances, couples might be found kissing in shadowy staircases or in the backseats of their parked cars. In a *New York Times* article, journalist Helen Bullitt Lowry notes how one sixteen-year-old flapper explained to her mother that her friends from school shared stories about having "put out." "'Put out!' gasped her puzzled mother. 'What does put out mean?' 'Oh, kissed the boys and things like that,' explained our flapper, casually, 'put out petting, you know.'"[10]

Such disregard for traditional modesty and decorum greatly concerned many members of the older generation. Schools and churches adopted programs to curb what was characterized as immoral behavior. For example, school officials brought in chaperones to supervise parties and dances. Hoping that modest dress would make young, single women less alluring to men, leaders of fifteen Protestant denominations agreed that clergy should recommend that girls wear a loose-fitting dress with sleeves below the elbow and a hem that was no more than seven and a half inches from the floor. State legislators in Utah, Ohio, and Virginia went even further, passing bills forbidding women from wearing skirts that ended more than three inches above the ankle or blouses or dresses that showed more than three inches of the throat. Some social commentators even denounced the use of automobiles by young people, saying that the seclusion afforded by a car encouraged petting. None of these efforts, however, greatly affected the behavior of young women, who seemed not to care what their elders thought.

Exactly how seriously their elders needed to take the flappers' sexual attitudes is open to question, however. Historian Lois W. Banner observes that young women themselves did not really know what to make of their newfound freedom: "It meant, on the one hand, attending countless college proms and weekends; on the other, an aversion to any rules."[11] In any case, statistics show that during the 1920s the rate of marriage in the United States remained unchanged, and the reported number of out-of-wedlock pregnancies did not rise.

Smoking, Drinking, and Dancing

Yet flappers did shock their elders with their sexual openness; they also unnerved society by smoking cigarettes in public. At the time, the health risks of smoking were largely unknown, but smoking was for the most part accepted behavior only among men. For this reason, their use of cigarettes became another symbol of young women's rejection of tradition. For some women, in fact, smoking was a way of publicly stating their desire for equality with men. Like other practices flappers adopted, public smoking quickly spread beyond this smaller group of women. A survey in the late 1920s showed that 80 percent of college-age women approved of smoking not just for men but for women. Even authority figures often gave at least tacit approval to smoking. For example, one eastern women's college, Bryn Mawr, allowed students to smoke on campus; other colleges allowed smoking in the areas just outside the campus proper. Such tolerance, however, was not universal: Midwestern and southern colleges still barred smoking by women on or even near campus.

Not only did the young women openly smoke, but they also drank. The Eighteenth Amendment to the U.S. Constitution, prohibiting the sale of liquor, had been passed at the beginning of the 1920s, but Prohibition did not succeed in stopping the flow of beer, wine, and liquor. People might not be able to legally purchase or drink alcohol, but private drinking places, called speakeasies, admitted a select clientele. In these illegal establishments young women could be found standing at the bar drinking with the men. Flappers also attended dances and there they drank illicit liquor offered by their male companions, who carried it in flasks in their hip pockets. Like public smoking, drinking became commonplace among more people than just the flappers. Allen notes that drinking and sexual experimentation seemed inevitably to go together:

> There were stories of daughters of the most exemplary parents getting drunk—"blotto," as their companions cheerfully put it—on the contents of the hip-flasks of the new prohibition regime, and going out joyriding with men at four in the morning. And worst of all, even at well-regulated dances they were said to retire where the eye of the most sharp-sighted chaperon could not follow, and in darkened rooms or in parked cars to engage in the unspeakable practice of petting and necking.[12]

Two flappers enjoy drinks in a speakeasy. Smoking and drinking, activities traditionally reserved for men, became common among young women of the 1920s.

Young women further violated social norms at public gatherings. At dances they no longer glided gracefully about in stately dances like waltzes. Instead, the flappers danced the bunny hug, the turkey trot, and the Charleston as ensembles blared jazz music, often accompanied by vocalists singing highly suggestive lyrics. Allen describes the bunny hug, saying: "No longer did even an inch of space separate [the couple]; they danced as if glued together, body to body, cheek to cheek."[13] The Charleston, which required fast, fancy footwork, was a wild dance. Barrett describes a flapper doing the Charleston: "Loose elbows, loose knees, feet flying, beads flying, slave bracelets ajangle. It doesn't make much sense, but brother, it's fun."[14]

Trifles and Ballyhoo

Young women displayed a defiant spirit with their nontraditional clothing styles and by flouting society's behavioral norms; this defiance was emblematic of a basic rejection of their elders' seriousness

A couple dances the Charleston in a 1926 dance contest. Wildly popular, the Charleston involved fast dance steps and unconventional moves.

of purpose and work ethic. Instead, young women directed their attention on celebrities, competitions, and sensational events, all of which were focused more on fun than on serious study and preparation for adult duties. Newspapers, in pursuit of readers, devoted much space to sensational stories. The events and disproportionate publicity came to be known as trifles and ballyhoo. Thanks to

such coverage, an obsession with trivial and sensational events soon spread across America.

The stories of seemingly outrageous behavior both repelled and riveted readers of newspapers. For example, young women across America were fascinated by the story of Frances Heenan and "Daddy" Browning. At fifteen, Peaches, as she was known, married a fifty-one-year-old real

Women of the Roaring Twenties

Flappers Invade the Barber Shop

Flappers wanted equality with men. One way of pursuing equality was to have their hair cut in men's barbershops. In a *New York Times* article, "Bobbing Spreads to All Ages of Women," published on May 11, 1924, Virginia Pope tells how women's presence changed barbershops. Her article is reprinted in *Women: Their Changing Roles*, edited by Elizabeth Janeway.

Not so long ago the men reclined in their barber chairs, gazing over lathered cheeks at maidens hurrying past the plate-glass window with downcast eyes. They felt secure in their collarless isolation. But times have changed. The up-to-date barber shops now have special chairs for women, and the women, true to the ways of today, take their places beside the men.

"Oh, yes," said the manager of a Broadway hotel barber shop, "we do many ladies here every day. Some come for bobs, some for trims. A beautiful young woman walked in the other day and wanted to have her hair cut off. I shudderingly watched the barber apply his clips to her long black curls. Before the operation was completed I was called from the room. When I returned I looked for the transformation. The girl was nowhere to be seen. I asked one of the barbers and he pointed to a sheeted form stretched out in a chair. On either side of her were similar figures, all with mud packs pasted over their faces. I couldn't tell the women from the men. Her hair, like theirs, was short. My eyes wandered to the tips of her shoes. 'Well,' said I to myself, 'this mannish business has gone to her head. Thank goodness, she can't change her feet!'"

Many flappers like this woman went to men's barbershops to have their hair cut in a short bob style.

estate baron named Edward Browning, who had wooed her with gifts and flowers. After a few months of marriage, Peaches discovered that Browning was in the habit of such nonconventional behavior as wandering about the house in the nude. When Browning insisted that his young wife join in such activities, Peaches fled. She then filed for divorce. Because Browning refused to go along with the divorce, the case resulted in a court trial, which the newspapers reported on day after day. Readers loved the lurid details of this young woman's brief marriage. When she was asked by a journalist why she had married Browning, her answer, "I haven't the faintest idea,"[15] epitomized the frivolous attitude toward life that prevailed among flappers.

Stories like the one about Peaches Heenan competed for readers' attention with stories about Hollywood celebrities. Writer Paul Sann notes that movie idol Rudolph Valentino "with the classic features and the bedroom eyes had so much appeal that he utterly enslaved the female movie-goers. . . . For the girls, no other celluloid [film] hero, before or after, would match Valentino's boundless magnetism. He became the Flapper's dreamboat."[16] Even death could not diminish Valentino's appeal. When the movie star died unexpectedly in 1926 after a four-day illness, crowds of women thronged to see his body lying in state. Newspa-

pers all across the country carried detailed accounts of the funeral and ran pictures of grief-stricken young women passing by their idol's coffin.

For flappers and young women in general, Valentino had clear sexual appeal. Charles Lindbergh, meanwhile, who was the first person to fly solo, nonstop across the Atlantic Ocean in 1927, represented a different sort of dream: the clean-cut boy next door who almost any young girl could imagine herself marrying. Young women followed every word of the newspaper accounts of his flight and his reception by masses of French men and women upon his landing in Paris. When Lindbergh returned to the United States, young women sent letters and presents to the young aviator, and many offered to marry him. Barrett says, "For the returning Colonel Lindbergh there [was] a mail call of two million letters, 100,000 telegrams of congratulations, 14,000 presents, and thousands of proposals of marriage."[17]

At the same time, young women idolized other young women who showed their independence and succeeded in accomplishing tasks equal to those of men. For example, in 1926 Gertrude Ederle swam the English Channel in fourteen hours and thirty-one minutes, nearly an hour and a half faster than any man had swum it. Even men were awed by Ederle: New York City's mayor, Jimmy

Walker, joined in the adulation of Ederle, comparing her crossing to other great historical feats: "Moses crossing the Red Sea, Caesar crossing the Rubicon and Washington crossing the Delaware."[18]

Competitions and Crimes

In addition to such stories about celebrities, newspapers captured young women's attention with reports on contests of various sorts. Newspapers ran accounts, for example, of beauty pageants. Contests such as the first Miss America pageant, held in 1921, in which participants were judged in part for how they looked in skin-tight bathing suits, fascinated women and men both. In keeping with rapidly changing views of what was appropriate public behavior, thousands of people watching such pageants either gasped or applauded when the scantily clad beauties paraded before them.

If some observers were shocked at the sight of women in bathing suits, others were astounded by such frivolous spectacles as dance marathons, the object of which was simply to see which couple could dance for the longest time

A weary couple struggles to keep moving during a 1929 dance marathon. The goal of such marathons was to be the last couple standing after hours and hours of dancing.

without stopping. The youthful participants, however, treated such contests with the utmost seriousness. Allen notes: "Marathon dancers clung to one another by the hour and day and week, shuffling about the floor in an agony of weariness."[19]

The Defiant Spirit

To satisfy the growing appetite for sensational stories of young women readers and an increasing adult audience, newspapers competed with one another to report odd behavior. Perhaps the most bizarre story was one about a flagpole-sitting contest in Baltimore. For more than three weeks, young women followed reports of Shipwreck Kelly, who wanted to set the record for the longest time that anyone sat on a perch at the top of a flagpole. He won the prize by sitting on the flagpole for twenty-three days and seven hours. Throughout the contest, the young women speculated each day whether or not he would come down. Newspapers encouraged such speculation and sold millions of copies as a result.

In their search for stories to boost sales, newspapers tried never to miss an opportunity to capitalize on frivolous attitudes. For example, violence and fashion dominated the stories about the Scopes trial, which involved a controversy about the teaching of evolution in a high-school biology class. Instead of reporting on the trial proceedings, newspapers used banner headlines to report on the fights that broke out between the crowds gathered outside the courtroom, either supporting or opposing the teaching of evolution. The most sensational event reported from inside the courtroom was the coverage of the judge's daughters, who came to watch the proceedings one day dressed as flappers. Allen reports, "Fashion was not wholly absent: the news was flashed over the wires to the whole country that the judge's daughters, as they entered the courtroom with him, wore rolled stockings like any metropolitan flapper's."[20]

As such attention to the trivial suggests, in the aftermath of cataclysms like World War I, American society was ready for a break when it exploded into the Roaring Twenties. The pace was fast, and much of what people did was frivolous. Young women, symbolized by the flapper, led the way. The flappers and their activities, however, represent just one element of life in the decade. Edwin L. James wrote of the flapper in the *New York Times*:

> Halt in her mad whirl the golden-dressed dancer who swings in magic circles as if to escape from herself. Look in her eyes, listen to her laughter, and you will find among her vain thoughts a strange fear, a sentiment of unrest, an almost crazy desire to forget yesterday, tomorrow, and herself.
>
> But this dancer is not the modern woman. She is only one of the aspects of modern women.[21]

Chapter 2:
Coeds and Housewives

W hile the flappers held the limelight in the Roaring Twenties and represented the wilder, more frivolous side of the decade, young women attending college displayed another aspect of what sociologists refer to as the New Woman. These were women who rejected the traditional view of a housewife as a submissive possession dedicated to keeping house and raising a family. Instead, the New Woman wanted a relationship that would place her more or less on equal terms with her husband. Rather than being merely a reflection of her husband's interests, this adult New Woman wanted to be a friend and partner to her husband. Woloch notes, too, that there was more than one kind of New Woman:

Despite the extensive publicity, the irrepressible flapper was hardly the only New Woman of the 1920s. On the contrary, she was more of a symbol of liberated attitudes and aspirations, promoted in the movies and the press and vividly imprinted on the popular memory. The decade in fact featured a variety of New Women: the campus coed, now imbued more with hopes of marriage than with a sense of mission; [and] the modern housewife, who adopted the role of companion and consumer.[22]

More Women Attend College

In a sense, the role of the campus coed served as an apprenticeship for the role of modern housewife. This was training that increasing numbers of young women were receiving, too. In the early 1920s, young women, especially those from the middle class, enrolled in colleges at a higher rate than ever before in history. In 1920 over 47 percent of all college students were women. The underlying reason for this increase was a new attitude among mothers and daughters. Mothers hoped that a college education would provide a variety of opportunities for their daughters. Mothers saw a college

College students gather together just before their graduation ceremony. For some women, college provided a chance to meet men they could marry.

education as essential both for becoming active participants in society and for preparing for any job young women might want to pursue. These mothers encouraged in their female offspring the belief that going to college was something they were expected to do. Young women had similar reasons for attending college. The more serious ones wanted to participate actively in life around them. They believed, as an August 22, 1920, article from the *New York Times* stated, "that college will give them contact with varieties of people representing varieties of opinion, tradition, character, and power, which will be valuable for their life as citizens."[23] They attended college because they wanted to do something useful and to achieve prominence in society.

The more common reason that women enrolled in college, however, was the opportunity it afforded for meeting the right man to marry. Though women hoped to play new, more significant roles in society than their mothers and grandmothers had, most of them still placed marriage ahead of other objectives. Author Anne Morrow Lindbergh was typical; she recalled that "she spent her time at Smith College and afterward in the classic manner of the bright college student: working hard at her studies, hoping to win the poetry prize, seeing numerous men, and fretting whether she would ever marry."[24]

College might have served as a sort of preparation for marriage, but historians Nancy F. Cott and Elizabeth H. Pleck note the seeming contradiction when a woman added child rearing to her wifely duties: "The colleges had taught them that it was better to read Plato than to wash diapers, to prefer a lecture on T.S. Eliot to staying at home with the babies."[25] Some educators dismissed the idea that a liberal arts degree somehow failed to prepare them for their roles as mothers. M. Carey Thomas, head of Bryn Mawr, said:

> Women cannot conceivably be given an education too broad, too high, or too deep to fit them to become the educated mothers of the future race of men and women born of educated parents. . . . They must think straight, judge wisely, reverence truth, and they must teach such clear and wise and reverent thinking to their children.[26]

Some colleges eliminated some of the contradiction by adding courses emphasizing domestic skills. In particular, land-grant universities, which had generally been established to teach young men to farm according to modern scientific principles, created departments of home economics, domestic science, and household administration. And during the 1924–1925 school year, the women's liberal arts college Vassar established the Institute of Euthenics, whose classes taught how improvement of human functioning could be achieved by improvement in living conditions; in other words, women could improve the lives of children and husbands by improving conditions at home.

Although courses emphasizing domestic skills taught young women how better to fill the role of wife and mother, it was at large state colleges and universities where women students created something like a social revolution. Now men and women approached each other nearly as equals. It was on these campuses that the idea of a woman entering a serious relationship as an equal of the man gained acceptance. Woloch notes: "The coed of the 1920s assumed the roles of 'pal' and 'partner,' both defined in terms of her relationship to men. Her dual role rested on the assumption that equality meant assuming the privileges and mannerisms once monopolized by men. It carried an aura of experimentation and innovation."[27]

The Coed's Role in Dating

The coeds of the 1920s transformed the practice of courtship from calling to dating. In the past a young man would have called on a young woman in her home in the presence of her family, but only after he had received an invitation from the

A female fan attends a 1923 Harvard football game. Going on dates to such events allowed college coeds to become acquainted with one another.

young lady to do so. In the 1920s on college campuses, however, couples dated. Usually, the man invited the woman to accompany him to a public event or function, such as a movie or sporting event. Women customarily dated a variety of men, not just one, and the most popular women often had dates every night of the week, or at least four or five dates a week.

The dating system offered women new freedoms. Couples who had access to automobiles were able to go to functions many miles from home. More importantly, they were free of family supervision. Consequently, they had more privacy to develop their relationships as they wished.

This new system of dating, however, did not necessarily empower women. Indeed, in one way they had less power than they had enjoyed in the past. Historian Beth L. Bailey says, "In the dating system, the woman became the man's guest in the public sphere, he paid for her entertainment, and thus she lost the power of initiative. Women did not ask men out on dates."[28]

Yet if the dating system took away one source of power, that loss was compensated by other freedoms. Banner notes:

"Freedom," defined in sexual and personal terms, was the new value. If young women wanted power and influence over men, they could get it by playing standard female roles: by being a temptress on the dance floor or a companion on the golf course. They could drink, they could smoke, they could enjoy sex.[29]

Because couples were unchaperoned, the coed's sexual behavior resembled that of the flapper's. Petting became a social ritual, which, as reported by Woloch, women viewed as "a substitute for more advanced sexual activity."[30] Though there were tales of a few college women participating in wild and reckless behavior, surveys showed that women were more restrained in their behavior than they let on. Moreover, pregnancy rates among college women increased by only a tiny percentage during the 1920s. According to some historians, the changes in sexual and personal behavior that came with the practice of dating helped prepare young women for their roles as adult women. Woloch says that "dating had indisputable influence on women's roles. It provided practice in the paired activities that would later be a way of life—basic training in the roles of 'pal' and 'partner.'"[31]

Coeds Popularize Sororities

Reinforcing the idea that a woman could or should be equal to a man in a marriage were college sororities. These organizations offered an alternative to dormitory accommodations, but were located very close to campus and were often closely supervised by college officials. In sororities, girls were expected to strive for an attractive appearance and to develop the social skills they needed in order to form compatible relationships with men. In other words, sororities promoted the role of pal and partner. Life in a sorority was imagined to help young women develop sex appeal and a pleasant personality.

Sororities were not, however, designed to mold just any young woman into the perfect mate. Membership in sororities was only by invitation from the active members. Most sororities, moreover, had restrictions based on color and religion; the actives, as they were known, saw nothing wrong with rejecting someone for being Jewish, for example, and it was unheard of in the 1920s for sororities to admit women of color. An applicant's command of etiquette was carefully evaluated, and preference was given to girls whose families were wealthy and socially accepted. Selection took place in a process called rushing, which usually occurred in the fall, shortly after classes began. Freshman girls applied to the sororities they hoped to join. During rush week, they attended parties held at the sorority houses. This gave the members a chance to observe the applicants' social skills. The actives voted on whether to admit or reject each applicant.

One woman dean of students noted that sororities tended "to select girls who dress well and rate well with men."[32] The members reasoned that a girl who rated well with men would attract a pool of attractive men to the sorority and give other members a better chance for dates. The net effect was for sororities to be self-perpetuating, choosing new members who closely mirrored those who would be graduating.

Sororities offered social activities and instruction in how to become the ideal wife-companion. They sponsored dances so that members could meet men who would make good husbands. Author Sheila M. Rothman enumerates the kinds of instruction provided to sorority girls:

> The sororities taught the girls about good appearance—how to apply cosmetics, how to bob hair, how much to shorten skirts. They instructed the girls in the talents of being good hostesses (later girls would know how to entertain their husband's friends and business associates). They gave practical lessons in playing bridge, in drinking, in smoking (all of which would fit the girls well for membership in the country clubs); they also defined the standards of sexual permissiveness—how far to go to interest a man (petting), without going too far.[33]

Adult New Women Transform Marriage

Sororities promoted the idea that women would one day become housewives who supported their husbands' aspirations, rather than wage earners themselves. These adult women, however, redefined their role within marriage by placing new emphasis on sexuality. Woloch says, "Indeed, middle-class married women were the unsung sexual revolutionaries of the early twentieth century. This gradual revolution had long-term repercussions, starting in the 1920s when marriage was redefined as a sexual institution."[34]

The adult New Woman, then, held higher expectations for what marriage offered than her mother and grandmother had held. The women of the 1920s expected marriage to be more than a series of obligations to a man. Dorothy Dunbar Bromley, writing in *Harper's Magazine*, says, "But even while she admits that a home and children may be necessary to her complete happiness, she will insist upon *more freedom and honesty within the marriage relation.*"[35] Women saw the new ideal for marriage as a romantic sexual union, more or less an extension of the dating she did in college. Professionals, such as sociologists, psychologists, and physicians, helped to define the new view of marriage, which appeared in textbooks, advice columns, and magazines.

Two young married couples enjoy a meal in a New York restaurant. Throughout the 1920s, married women redefined their roles as wives and mothers.

Woloch identifies several of these views: Marriage offers a woman a role "as lover and companion"; she can enjoy "a fuller and richer life" in marriage; and her marriage is an opportunity for "sharing joys and sorrows with a mate who will be not merely a protector and provider but an all round companion."[36]

Though women sought—and even gained—a measure of equality in marriage, the role of companion imposed some new obligations. For example, the pressure was on the wife to keep romance alive by maintaining a sexually attractive appearance. To do so, she employed the skills that she had learned in her sorority, such as maintaining an attractive haircut, applying makeup properly, and choosing a wardrobe that enhanced the shape of her body. Besides being attractive, she was expected to have an interesting personality so that her husband would not become bored. She could remain interesting by using her liberal arts education to initiate conversations involving ideas and events of the day. Moreover, she was expected to keep the right social contacts and organize a social life that kept her husband entertained. Fulfilling these expectations made being a housewife a full-time job. If she had children, she was expected to care for them as well.

A marriage in which the wife served as the supportive companion to her husband was the norm, but was by no means universal. Other couples tried a "semidetached" marriage, in which the husband and wife lived in the same house but kept parts of their lives independent and separate from their spouses. Feminist Crystal Eastman even claimed that she and her husband saved the romance in their marriage by living completely apart. With that arrangement, they said, they were not smothered by each other and were free to be together when they chose, not because they had to do so. Eastman wrote in the December 1923 issue of *Cosmopolitan* magazine:

> Perhaps divorce is the only remedy for difficult marriages. But if my theory is correct, if it is the too constant sharing of one home, with no easy and normal method of escape, which primarily makes them difficult, then some loosening of the time-and-space conventions so bound up with marriage is worth trying. Separate beds, separate rooms, have not done much to reconcile people to marriage. Why not take a bold romantic step and try separate roofs?[37]

Eastman claimed that the arrangement gave her and her husband one of the happiest periods of their marriage. Such experiments found little widespread support in the 1920s, but they worked for very independent-minded women whose husbands were willing to accommodate them.

Birth Control

Whatever the nature of a couple's living arrangements, women understood that the stress and sheer volume of work that childbearing involved meant that romance and large numbers of children were incompatible. Consequently, the issue of birth control was important for wives. For all practical purposes, birth control had been illegal since 1873, when Congress had passed the Comstock Law, forbidding the distribution of birth-control materials as well as information about contraception. Women campaigned all through the 1920s for changes so that information and materials to prevent pregnancies could be available.

Women also wanted birth control because they believed that freedom from worry about pregnancy would improve their marriages and their lives in general. Crystal Eastman wrote in *The Birth Control Review*:

> We want to love and be loved, and most of us want children, one or two

at least. But we want our love to be joyous and free—not clouded with ignorance and fear. And we want our children to be deliberately, eagerly called into being, when we are at our best, not crowded upon us in times of poverty and weakness. We want this precious sex knowledge not just for ourselves, the conscious feminists; we want it for all the millions of unconscious feminists that swarm the earth,—and we want it for all women.[38]

As Eastman implied, for poor women, the effects on romance of having many children was the least of their worries. One woman told of living in two rooms with two beds for a family of seven. Another told of having three cots and a box to accommodate her eight children. For poor women, then, access to birth

Police Raid Birth-Control Meeting

❦

The *New York Times* reported on November 15, 1921, that the police arrested activists Margaret Sanger and Mary Winsor just after they had taken the stage at the first American Birth Control Conference. At the time, birth control and distributing information about it were illegal. The article is reprinted in Janeway's *Women: Their Changing Roles.*

Mrs. Margaret Sanger and Mary Winsor, who were arrested at the meeting when they attempted to speak, by the order of Captain Donohue, were discharged yesterday by Magistrate Joseph E. Corrigan for lack of evidence. Following their release they went into conference with counsel to determine what legal steps would be taken to prevent police interference at further meetings and to obtain redress for the action taken Sunday.

The first American Birth Control Conference, which had arranged Sunday's meeting as part of the program of a three days' conference, announced yesterday that the meeting would be held on Friday night at Bryant Hall, Forty-second Street and Sixth Avenue. The subject will be "Birth Control: Is It Moral?" and the speakers will be Mrs. Sanger and Harold Cox, a former member of the British Parliament, who had come here from England to speak at the Town Hall.

control was more than just a lifestyle issue.

The New Woman as Consumer

For middle-class women, at least, smaller families also meant that they spent less time on household chores. At the same time, advances in technology were bringing dozens of time- and labor-saving products within reach of people of even modest means. Electric irons, vacuum cleaners, and washing machines all became more widely available. Also, the greatly increased availability of canned fruits and vegetables and other prepared food items allowed many middle-class women to spend far less time in the kitchen than ever before. Now women assumed the roles of shopper and manager of the household budget and shed the role of hardworking drudge. Freed of the most physically demanding chores, housewives at least had a chance to be more active partners in their marriages.

The image of housewives as happy consumers was defined and encouraged by the advertising industry. Advertisers, especially those who marketed their products in *Ladies' Home Journal*, the most popular women's magazine, played into women's desire to have a romantic marriage. "National advertising," commented sociologist Ernest Brugess, "utilizes sex as perhaps its most enticing lure in baiting the attention of the buying public to its wares."[39] Ads in the magazine implied that any woman who failed to use personal-care products would lose sex appeal and popularity. If she did not use Listerine, for example, she would have bad

An advertisement from 1925 shows a housewife preparing a meal in her kitchen equipped with the latest appliances.

breath; the implication was that she would fail to find a husband. A deodorant ad promised a woman that she could be as sweet as a rose and that only "with an underarm dry at all times can she be sure . . . she will be immaculate in low-cut evening gowns."[40] Advertisers, who up to this point had relied on straightforward recitation of facts to sell their products, found success by suggesting that they could help women achieve the ideal of being a successful homemaker and a desirable sexual partner.

Historians note that advertisers went a step further by not only appealing to women's romantic aspirations but also shaping those aspirations. Banner notes that "women were shown as beings for whom fashion, beauty, and sex appeal were the most important concerns in life."[41] Advertisers then went on to foster a sense of guilt if a woman failed to live up to the ideal. Social historian Ruth Schwartz Cowan notes, "More guilt and embarrassment about their failure to succeed at their work meant a greater likelihood that they would buy the products that were intended to minimize that failure."[42]

Of course, the image of the ideal wife and mother created by advertisers was

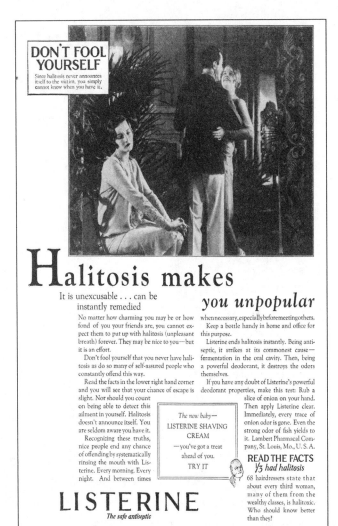

A Time *magazine ad warns that women with bad breath run the risk of being unpopular. Using Listerine, the ad implies, helps women attract suitable mates.*

only one aspect of the New Woman of the Roaring Twenties. The New Woman reflected some of the frivolity flappers portrayed. In addition, the New Woman embodied a seriousness of purpose that was particularly evident among women in the performing arts.

Chapter 3:
Women Performers

❧

Whereas flappers rebelled against social norms and housewives sought greater equality in their marriages, women who played prominent roles in classical music, theater, dance, jazz, and film worked hard to redefine their place in these artistic arenas. In classical music, women insisted on being taken seriously as artists capable of playing in the top orchestras. On Broadway, women confidently accepted roles in new, experimental plays. Dancers abandoned the rigidly defined movements of classical ballet in favor of forms that looked more natural. Jazz and blues singers performed songs whose lyrics were openly sexual in character. Film stars took cues from the flapper's image of social rebel and made that image even more daring. The twenties, then, was a vibrant and experimental decade in which women performing artists took risks as never before.

Classical Music Performers

Though male composers such as Aaron Copland and Charles Ives dominated the composition of classical music, women composers also found ways of getting their works performed in the 1920s. For example, Mabel Wheeler Daniels, who had been director of music at Simmons College in Boston, composed a work titled *Symphony Exaltate;* its innovative form and themes earned her a reputation as one of the finest composers of the time. Daniels was frequently interviewed about her music and always asked to comment about the scarcity of women composers. Frustrated by the widely held belief that women could not compose large, serious musical works, she asserted that music is music, no matter who composes it: "What difference whether [a work is] written by a man or a woman or a Hottentot [a tribe in southern Africa] or a Unitarian [a religious denomination that stresses reason over faith]."[43]

As was true of composers, most concert pianists in the 1920s were male, but a few women managed to gain the attention of concertgoers, overcoming the preference among the men who scheduled performances in concert halls for male musicians. For example, Hazel Harrison toured America playing the music of Strauss, Bach, Liszt, and the works of unpublished black composers. Harrison had to contend with a second barrier since she was African American and therefore was often not allowed to perform for white audiences. For example, after a Harrison recital in Chicago in 1922, a reviewer said, "She is extremely talented . . . it seems too bad that the fact that she is a Negress may limit her future plans."[44] White women found themselves more readily accepted. For example, another pianist, Ethel Leginska, was compared favorably to Ignace Jan Paderewski, a renowned Polish pianist and composer. Leginska not only performed on the piano but conducted orchestras in London, Paris, Munich, Berlin, and New York. In 1926 she founded the Boston Woman's Symphony and later went on to direct the Woman's Symphony of Chicago.

Less groundbreaking than women composers, conductors, and musicians were those who sang opera. European women had for centuries been filling female roles in operas, but American singers, because of a prevailing disregard for women's talent and intelligence, were rarely encouraged to train for the most demanding vocal careers. In the early 1920s, American singers gained experi-ence singing other kinds of music before they performed in major opera houses. For example, Grace Moore sang lyrics written by Irving Berlin in *Music Box Review* at a Broadway theater before she landed a role in 1928 at the Metropolitan Opera, where she sang the leading role of Mimi in the opera *La Boheme.* Another singer, Rosa Ponselle, trained in New York and sang in churches and in vaudeville acts until her extraordinary voice caught the attention of the famous opera star Enrico Caruso. Dorothy Brown cites a turning point in Ponselle's career: "In 1927, her performance in [the opera] *Norma* established her as one of the great sopranos of the century."[45] She went on to sing many leading roles opposite Caruso.

Contributions to Theater

In addition to their contributions to classical music, women made major contributions to theater in the 1920s by using the same persistence and spirit as women who succeeded on the concert stage. Especially in New York, which was a gathering place for American playwrights, women worked to bring new talent to the attention of theatergoers. Theresa Helburn, for example, took charge of the Theatre Guild, an organization that produced plays. She aggressively solicited new dues-paying members for the guild, swelling its ranks to

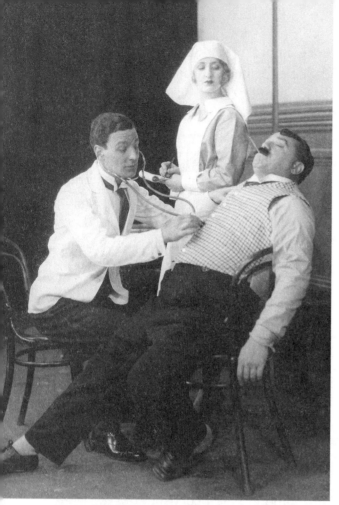

A photograph shows a scene from a 1929 vaudeville play. Vaudeville and other theaters offered female performers the opportunity to perform on stage.

twenty-five thousand. Thanks to her efforts, funds were available to produce serious new plays written by struggling playwrights. Helburn received support from the editor of *Theater Arts* magazine, Edith Isaacs, who recruited talented actors and promoted them for roles in the plays Helburn helped to produce. Another promoter was Susan Glaspell; with her hus-

band George Cran Cook, she formed the Greenwich Village Playwrights Theater, whose mission was to produce original American plays. In addition to putting on plays, Glaspell wrote them. Her best-known play, *Trifles*, became a part of the standard reading list for students of literature.

Women who promoted plays contributed to the general quality of theater, but many women impacted the theater scene by performing. These women often made their way onto the stage by performing in popular shows like the Ziegfeld Follies and vaudeville. The Ziegfeld Follies was a show put on annually that consisted of skits, stand-up comedy, and satire. One of the stars of the Follies was Fanny Brice, who excelled at comedy. According to Brown, Brice could do "a sidesplitting takeoff on [movie] vamp Theda Bara or on [the ballet role of] the Dying Swan."[46]

Vaudeville offered more opportunities to African American women than either classical music or theater did. Vaudeville often featured African Americans in stereotypical submissive roles such as maids. Still, vaudeville offered black women more opportunities to perform, since this was one art form in which both black and white audiences accepted black performers. One of the stars of vaudeville was Josephine Baker. After playing in the musical review titled *Shuffle Along* on Broadway, she struck out on her own and took her vaudeville show *La Revue Negre* to Paris. Parisians rejected her show for having too much tap dancing, but it won her a dancing role in the Folies Bergère, a Paris dance theater. Because the audience reacted to her dancing with such great enthusiasm, Baker left the theater and created a one-woman show, which she performed in Paris. One critic was so impressed that he likened her to a Greek goddess and called her the "Black Venus."[47]

In addition to vaudeville, women performed as leading ladies in serious plays produced on Broadway in New York City. The decade saw a large number of strong, talented women performing serious roles in plays by American playwrights Eugene O'Neill and Thornton Wilder and in works by English and European playwrights, including Henrik Ibsen, Anton Chekhov, and William Shakespeare. A long list of famous stars included Ethel Barrymore, Helen Hayes, and Lynn Fontanne. The outstanding star, however, was Katharine Cornell, who one critic said had a "radiance" about her: "To see her in action or to talk to her at leisure is to note the perpetual presence of the indwelling, fiery guest that it is her destiny to harbor while she is on this earth."[48] By giving outstanding performances in serious plays, these talented women contributed to the success of Broadway during the 1920s.

Women Dancers

Women who wished to dance were fortunate in that dance was an art form in which they found acceptance and the freedom to innovate. The earlier decades of the twentieth century were a time when dance usually meant classical ballet, in which women performed a number of graceful movements and spun delicately on their toes while their male partners performed athletically challenging leaps that showcased their agility and strength. During the 1920s, however, two women founded essentially a new art form, what has become known as modern dance. Martha Graham was one of these innovators. Graham's career passed through several stages, during which she taught dance, performed in small-group recitals, and managed her own dance studio. Eventually, she created entire programs, such as *Primitive Mysteries* and *Appalachian Spring*. She was a woman with a big vision and an important goal for dance, as Graham herself said, "to affirm the universal experiences of humankind"[49] and to fulfill that vision with graceful yet highly physical movements. Bette Davis, who before gaining fame as a film actress had been a pupil of Graham's, captures her former teacher's talent:

> I worshipped her. She was all tension—lightning. Her burning dedication gave

her spare body the power of ten men. ... She was a straight line—a divining rod ... who would, with a single thrust of her weight, convey anguish. Then, in an anchored lift that made her ten feet tall, she became all joy. One after the other. Hatred, ecstasy, age, compassion! ... What at first seemed "grotesque to the eye" developed into a beautiful release for both dancer and beholder.[50]

Though Graham had the greatest influence on twentieth-century dance, another woman actually pioneered the modern-dance style. Even before Graham began her career, Isadora Duncan had redefined the meaning of dance. Duncan believed that dancers' movements should reflect those seen in nature. For example, she observed how flowers unfold and how bees fly and practiced moves that emulated these free and graceful motions. Duncan was fascinated by ancient Greek theater and designed costumes and moves that evoked images of Greece's Golden Age, when a chorus consisting of dancers accompanied the

Martha Graham dances with a male partner during a 1926 performance. During the 1920s, Graham helped to develop what is today known as modern dance.

actors on stage with physical interpretations of emotion. The result was an onstage style that took audiences by surprise. For example, during a performance at Carnegie Hall in New York City, Duncan leapt from the back of the stage, barefoot, clothed in filmy silk. Dancing to the music of Wagner, Beethoven, and Tchaikovsky, she seemed, according to one critic, to be a creature out of nature. For Duncan, this freedom of artistic expression was part of the larger struggle by women for equal rights. Duncan noted, "If my art is symbolic of any one thing, it is symbolic of the freedom of woman and her emancipation."[51]

Jazz and Blues

The world of dance, however, like almost all of the American art scene during the 1920s, was rigidly segregated. Therefore, although African American performers, like their white counterparts, wanted some control over their artistic lives, such control was rarely possible. In the American social hierarchy of the 1920s, black women had the least power. They had neither financial nor political freedom, and men, both white and black, expected them to be submissive. In blues songs, however, black women were able to express their longing for freedom in vivid lyrics. The power to choose or reject their partners was a favorite theme in the songs they wrote and sang. In these songs black

women sang of travel, which was a metaphor for freedom. Women could travel freely in their imaginations even when they were unable to do so in reality. In these songs, women walk, run, leave, catch trains, or amble aimlessly.

"Ma" Rainey

Two women created and popularized the blues songs with these themes during the decade of the 1920s. Gertrude "Ma" Rainey is called by many the Mother of the Blues. In her early career, she developed a collection of her own songs in her downtime from her traveling and teaching jobs. She began singing in tent shows in the South and then moved to Chicago. She married Will Rainey, who managed F.C. Woolcott's Rabbit-Foot Minstrel Group, and traveled with him. While in Chicago, however, she taught and supported numerous African American singers while she was developing her own blues songs.

Rainey's songs express a woman's independence and assertiveness in realistic, sometimes harsh, words. For example, in "Sweet Rough Man," Rainey sings of a woman who tolerates abuse because her man is a good lover, but in her mind she is free to choose to stay with him: "Lord, it ain't no maybe bout my man bein' rough/But when it comes to lovin', he sure can strut his stuff."[52] "Lawd, Send Me a Man Blues" is a straightforward plea

To the French, "Black is Beautiful"

Dancer Josephine Baker took a variety show to Paris and became a celebrity there. Though her original show was only marginally successful, she became a star dancer in the Folies Bergère. In *Harlem in Montmartre*, William A. Shack describes her celebrity status and the exotic role Baker played in it.

Baker's fame as an international celebrity benefited from the discovery by the French, long before anyone else, that black is beautiful. Hinri Varna, director of the Folies Bergère, realized the marketing possibilities of including an exotic black act in his show. Baker had that potential. Under his direction she became one of the Folies Bergère's most sensational successes. Swinging her elegant brown body to blues music was of less consequence than the newsworthy persona she created of her public life. Indeed, everything about Baker was newsworthy. Her gold fingernails led the comtesse Mathieu de Noailles (a socialite and, some said, France's greatest poet) to christen her "the pantheress with golden claws." For her leopard, Chiquita, Baker bought a different collar to match each of her dresses; snakeskin upholstered her chauffeur-driven Delage limousine. Women imitated her close-cropped slicked-down hairstyle and bought trademarked products *pour se bakerfixer les cheveux* [so that their hair could resemble Baker's]. At Deauville, a whole vogue of sunbathing was created by women trying to emulate her caramel skin color.

Josephine Baker became a huge star as a performer in Paris.

Blues singer Ma Rainey, seen in this 1923 photo with members of her Georgia Jazz Band, sang of travel and women's independence.

from a lonely woman who wants a man: "Send me a Zulu, a voodoo, any old man/I'm not particular, boys, I'll take what I can."[53] Rainey also explored women's desire for independence in songs that incorporate travel themes in their lyrics. For example, in "Traveling Blues," set in a train station, she sings of leaving because her man has chosen another woman: "I'm dangerous and blue, can't stay here no more/Here comes my train, folks, and I've got to go."[54] Whether her songs relate to men or to travel, Ma Rainey's works expressed a desire for independence among black women. She touched the hearts of women wherever she sang and garnered a popular following.

Bessie Smith

Blues singer Bessie Smith patterned herself after Rainey and expressed the same themes of independence for black women. Smith became better known and more popular than Rainey. She started her career as a blues singer in Harlem, just when this African American community was undergoing a cultural blossoming known as the Harlem Renaissance. Smith became the first African

Bessie Smith became the first African-American superstar and was revered for her versatile voice.

Like Rainey, Smith sang about love, sex, and travel. She expresses the power of seduction in "Lookin' for My Man Blues": "He's a red hot papa, melt hearts as cold as ice/Girls, if he ever love you once, you bound to love him twice."[56] Smith also sang about travel, as in "Louisiana Low Down Blues," which deals with a woman's freedom to leave: "Got a low down feelin', I can't lose my heavy load/My home ain't up North, it's further down the road."[57] Smith also gave advice to women, as "Preachin' the Blues" illustrates: "I ain't here to try to save your soul/Just want to teach you how to save your good jelly roll."[58] Rainey and Smith both sang boldly and alluringly about women's real-life experiences, and in so doing they helped elevate that status of other black women.

Both Rainey and Smith took advantage of new technologies. The most important new technology was recording equipment. Recordings captured the full impact of blues songs, whose meaning depended so much on the subtleties of the singer's voice. In the past, blues songs were available in the form of sheet music, which could not convey the emotion a talented singer added. In all, Rainey made 92 recordings, and Smith made 160. Smith's recordings were popular with both black and white crowds; she sold so many records that she became a rich woman.

American superstar. She developed a reputation as the "Empress of the Blues" because she could vary her voice from a majestic and operatic sound to a coarse and raspy rumble. Author John Fordham says her voice "could suggest a Baptist choir or a growling gutbucket trumpet."[55]

The Film Industry

Except for those who made records, even popular blues singers could project their sensuality to only a relatively small audience—rarely more than a few hundred at a time during a concert. Movies, though, allowed an actress or actor to convey an overtly sexual message to millions. One of the most popular roles in film was the sexually seductive temptress. Movie stars took the sexual allure of the flapper and made it seem attainable for the masses. For example, Clara Bow was a movie star who movie commentator Elinor Glyn called the "It Girl" as a way of putting a label on her indefinable sex appeal. Peter Sann says her appeal was indeed definable:

> It went back to the discarding of the ankle-length skirt and the high-buttoned shoe and the burlap-bag undergarment. Now it was better advertised and not a sin but a virtue. Now it marked the woman's total emancipation; the shackles were off. The "It Girl" had the same sex appeal as before but more of it was showing, and it was also a little more available. That was the point.[59]

Part of Clara Bow's allure was in the daringly revealing costumes she wore. She was like the flapper in that she pursued her man, but she was more bold and always succeeded in getting him.

Other filmstars injected more than a hint of illicit sex into their performances. For example, Theda Bara was the stereotype vamp, or temptress. So palpable was a sense of something forbidden in her performances that Bara was billed as the "wickedest force in the world."[60] Bara had black hair and enhanced her sexual allure with scanty, sheer costumes. She also was the first movie star to wear eye makeup, which the cosmetics entrepreneur Helena Rubinstein created especially for her.

Popular Stereotypes

Besides the seductive temptress, film actresses popularized other stereotypes in the early twenties. They did this by playing the same role over and over again. For example, Lillian Gish played the stereotypical orphan, too delicate, too good, and too sweet to survive in a complex world. One critic said that from the beginning of one of her films, "there is the feeling of inevitable doom. Too good for this world's pain, her only hope of happiness appears in death or the cloister."[61]

Whereas Lillian Gish played the part of the good orphan, Mary Pickford repeatedly played the role of a good adolescent just about to mature. She was called the "Girl with the Curl" because she was covered with blond curls. While in her twenties, for example, she played Rebecca of *Rebecca of Sunnybrook Farm* and Pollyanna. Pickford tried to break out of this stereotype of the good and active adolescent, but her fans refused to accept her in other roles. A *Photoplay* magazine survey indicated that 99 percent of respondents wanted her to play young heroines exclusively. By that time, even though she was thirty-two, she was still playing the part of a teenage heroine, in the movie *Little Annie Rooney*.

More Complex Roles for Women

The late twenties, however, offered women the chance to play roles that were more complex in films with more involved plots and greater character development. Two women in particular starred in these more sophisticated movies. One was Greta Garbo, who regularly starred with John Gilbert. In the minds of moviegoers, they were as inseparable a pair of lovers as Shakespeare's immortal characters Romeo and Juliet and Anthony and Cleopatra. Gloria Swanson played in movies produced by Cecil B. DeMille, who demanded that she project a complex persona onscreen. According to Brown, DeMille expected women in his films to perform with "torrid passion, generally in a dream or foreign or historic sequence, while managing to uphold traditional morality. Unlike the stereotypes of the orphan or the

Movies and the Flapper

Movies did much to promote the sensuality and glamour of the flapper, as Marvin Barrett notes in his book *The Jazz Age.*

"Go to a motion picture . . . and let yourself go," the ads urge, and America responds with 40 million paid admissions per week. "Before you know it you are *living* the story—laughing, loving, hating, struggling, winning! All the adventure, all the romance, all the excitement you lack in your daily life

are in—Pictures. They take you completely out of yourself into a wonderful new world. . . . Out of the cage of everyday existence! If only for an afternoon or an evening—escape!"

And what will you see when you get there? "Brilliant men, beautiful jazz babies, champagne baths, midnight revels, neckers, petters, white kisses, red kisses, pleasure-mad daughters, sensation-craving mothers . . . the Truth—bold, naked, sensational."

Actress Gloria Swanson appears in the 1927 film, The Loves of Sunya. *Under the direction of Cecil B. DeMille, Swanson played extremely complex onscreen characters.*

vamp, Swanson had to project a multi-dimensional role—sexual passion on one hand and traditional morality on the other. Swanson was a perfect actress for this duality."[62] In 1925 she starred in a DeMille movie called *Don't Change Your Husband* while she was beginning her third marriage.

As talented as they might be, women film stars of the 1920s generally did not try to project an aura of independence and equality with men. Their professional lives, after all, were in the hands of producers and directors, who all were male and who

were seldom inclined to tolerate opposition from any of their employees.

In no field of entertainment did women actually achieve equality with men in terms of pay or control over their professional lives. Yet these performers were still very influential. Women from all walks of life in one way or another found themselves looking to the performing artists of the day for guidance in the clothes they wore, the makeup they used, even what they looked for in a mate. In short, women entertainers helped define the New Woman.

Chapter 4:
Women in Business
and the Professions

The New Woman who wanted a career in business or one of the professions faced obstacles and conflicting messages. On the one hand, the traditions of male-dominated society suggested that women were incapable of demanding careers, yet women knew that they had talent and brains and so had plenty to contribute. Moreover, many women had gone to college and wanted to continue being challenged. The flapper might be leading a social revolution, but many women wanted the satisfaction of a serious career. Barbara J. Harris notes the dilemma of women with career goals:

> The whole significance of the 1920s is epitomized by the fact that the symbol of the decade was not the emancipated career woman, but the flapper. Although she was sexually liberated and had greater social freedom than her predecessors, the flapper fit easily into a society that saw women in predominantly sexual terms. When her dancing and drinking days were over, she settled down as wife and mother.[63]

The attitude that women should be satisfied with the role of wife and mother was definitely an obstacle to establishing a career. As was true of earlier times, women were encouraged to think of homemaking and the rearing of children as a complicated and noble full-time calling. In reality, however, housework had become simpler during the 1920s with the advent of the many new labor-saving appliances. Women had more time on their hands and, consequently, felt unchallenged. One midwestern housewife said, "Housework as a life job bores and enrages me."[64] Women who wanted careers were torn between fulfilling society's expectations and their own inclinations.

In any case, society's expectations meant that women had little hope of attaining a top management position in a large company. Among the men who made hiring decisions, the widely held view was that women lacked the aptitude for management. Moreover, this idea guaranteed that women had little, if any, opportunity to learn the skills needed by managers. The specifics of how to hire and motivate employees could be learned, but rarely did anyone think to teach those to women workers. Powerful men in business tended to believe that women lacked initiative, could not handle responsibility, and had frequent absences. Even some women held this attitude, as historian Grace Coyle wrote in 1928: "It is not assumed that they [women] have the calibre for executive positions. . . . The fact that they are likely to marry and leave the business also tends to keep them out of positions which are regarded as training for the higher levels."[65]

Male executives used these same unfounded beliefs to justify paying the women that they did hire less. In the 1920s there was no such thing for women as equal pay for equal work. Even when women did the same work as men, such as teaching high school, women received smaller salaries. It was common for women to be paid one-half to two-thirds of what men earned for comparable or identical work.

In facing such discrimination in the business world, women received no support even from organizations that had

In this 1925 photo, a group of women make ledger entries in an office. Throughout the decade, women routinely received smaller salaries than their male counterparts.

earlier been so intent on advocating for women's rights. The women's movement had, for all intents and purposes, collapsed after the passage of the Nineteenth Amendment, which had granted women the right to vote. With this right assured, many women thought that the work of feminists was completed. Feminist Anna Howard Shaw was also of the opinion that the very nature of the business world would work against a collective effort to end discrimination:

> You younger women will have a harder task than ours [gaining the right to vote]. You will want equality in business and it will be even harder to get than the vote, for you will have to fight for it as individuals and that will not get you far. Women will not unite, since they will be competitors with each other. As soon as a woman has it for herself she will have entered the man's world and cease to fight as a woman for other women.[66]

Faced with these discouraging conditions, many women struggled with the decision of whether or not to seek a career. Historian Frank Stricker captures the complexity facing women when he notes: "It must be full of the twists and turns, tensions and pragmatic decisions which constituted the story of thousands of women as they worked out their desire for a career and a personal life."[67]

In spite of the challenges, an increasing number of women chose careers throughout the decade. The circumstances, however, required that they compromise by abandoning hopes of advancement and settling for lower-level jobs. The result was a workplace that took on some resemblance of home, as Woloch notes:

> Women viewed the world of commerce as a new frontier of female employment. As more young women entered office work, the field was reshaped to suit domestic ideals. A sexual division of labor in business transformed office work into service work—or "women's work." A man entering business was expected to be ambitious, aggressive, and competitive, so as to rise in the ranks, but not so the woman office worker. She was expected instead to be neat, clean, agreeable, and useful to others—qualities that would later suit her for home life as well.[68]

Careers in Large Companies

The highest-level careers for women in many businesses usually involved supporting the general company operations. For example, even when women held college degrees, companies hired them as

Women of the Roaring Twenties

receptionists. Though a receptionist's work did not require specialized skills, male managers called these jobs "professional" simply because the women had contact with the public. The telephone industry also hired a large number of women as switchboard operators, who were also considered "professional" because the operator had to keep track of a number of telephone connections at once. Indeed, the operator's job was demanding, if highly repetitive. In those days telephones had neither keypads nor dials; instead, callers rang the operator and told her the number to be rung. The operator then inserted a plug into the socket matching that number to complete the connection. Dorothy M. Johnson, a telephone operator in Whitefish, Montana, described her work:

There were no flashing lights on our switchboard. It had rows of black eyes each with a number under it. When a subscriber wanted to make a call, he ground a crank. The little black eye above his number flipped over and showed red. . . . The board was a vast expanse of eyes, with, at the base, a dozen or so pairs of plugs on cords for connecting and an equal number of keys for talking, listening, and ringing. On a busy day these cords were woven across the board in a constantly changing, confusing pattern.[69]

In 1922 a telephone operator works at an enormous switchboard. Many women found jobs as operators for telephone companies.

While receptionists and telephone operators interacted with a large number of fellow employees or customers, other women worked in close association with one person. Such jobs primarily consisted of stenography, which involved the manager—who was always male—dictating the content of business letters, which the stenographer would write down word for word. Such positions were considered professional, because the job required speed and utmost accuracy. Stenographers had prestige, often were granted paid vacations, and were paid relatively high wages. Rothman notes the advantages of these jobs:

> Women took over stenographic positions, mastering the skills of shorthand and learning to take dictation and then to type the letters. These were well-paying jobs, and women eagerly filled them; a typist earned $6 to $10 a week, a stenographer between $12 and $16. An income of $700 a year put a stenographer well up on the scale of earnings at a time when unskilled labor received about

$200 annually, and semi-skilled workers about $400 to $500.[70]

The better stenographers became indispensable to their bosses, who relied on them for additional tasks such as keeping track of appointments and running errands. Despite their specialized skills and significant responsibilities, stenographers and other women in offices were rarely credited with possessing an intellect. They were expected simply to be pretty and generously contribute to the morale of the office. In general, female office help became part of the businessman's perquisites, whether in small firms or large corporations. Journalist Lorine Pruette wrote in 1931, "The businessman

Female employees tend to customers in a New York department store. Such stores typically hired women as support staffers and window decorators.

begins to feel himself a success when he has a secretary. A girl feeds his vanity."[71]

Other women in business supported the company's financial department. These support jobs, which kept a company's financial operations running, were considered professional because women needed to be proficient and accurate in handling calculations. Small companies, in particular, hired women as bookkeepers, who recorded all of the monetary transactions of a company, including taking care of the payroll. Large companies hired women for more specialized financial duties. For example, a large firm might hire a woman just as a payroll clerk.

In business, then, women were never hired as decision makers; those jobs always went to men. Women might well be hired for jobs that were key to the business—for example, as tellers in banks, assisting customers with depositing or withdrawing money. But a bank would never put a woman in a decision-making job, such as a loan officer. Similarly, in department stores, which were increasing in number and size during the 1920s, women supported the male marketing managers. Women served as window decorators, setting up merchandise to highlight seasons and holidays, a job that was considered to be akin to homemaking.

In the absence of effective national organizations to protest against discrimination and lobby for legal protection, women in diverse occupations established their own support organizations. One such organization was the National Federation of Business and Professional Women's Clubs. Women in this organization and its smaller affiliates would meet to discuss wages and working conditions. They also served as places a woman could turn to for advice on dealing with a wide variety of workplace issues.

Women as Managers and Entrepreneurs

As the 1920s progressed, a few women succeeded in becoming managers. By 1930, for example, there were six female managers of small or medium-sized telephone companies. A woman named Mary Dillon, however, achieved one of the highest-level positions. She became the president of the Brooklyn Borough Gas Company, the first woman to head a major public utility company.

Though men doubted women's ability to manage large firms, society in general approved of women owning and managing specialty shops—as long as their merchandise did not compete with that offered by male-owned shops. Banner notes:

Often in the 1920s these businesswomen made their money by marketing products designed for women. Industries like fashion and retailing have always been relatively open to determined career women. And in those years shrewd female entrepreneurs recognized the immense potential of the market created by the new sex consciousness.[72]

Successful shops owned by women usually specialized in women's clothing. Such shops might offer the clothes worn by flappers or sell neat, professional styles appropriate for the office. In general, society approved of women owning shops that sold items that had a feminine quality about them. For example, women owned and managed successful shops that sold children's clothing; other types of shops considered appropriate businesses for women sold flowers, gifts, or greeting cards.

A few individuals, in fact, became highly successful by designing, producing, and marketing new products meant for women. For example, Hattie Carnegie developed a line of women's clothing. She had gotten her start working at Macy's Department Store in New York. Later, she teamed up with a seamstress named Rose Roth and began designing expensive hats and garments. Carnegie opened a clothing shop located on Riverside Drive, a fashionable district in New York City, where she marketed her clothes to wealthy women. By 1929 her designs had achieved such a reputation

that the "Carnegie Look" was a mark of prestige and she was bringing in sales of $3 million a year.

Another example of a successful woman entrepreneur was Madame C.J. Walker. While working as a washerwoman in the South, she had envisioned a procedure for straightening black women's hair, which was common practice at the time. Walker developed a system that consisted of shampoo, pomade (a perfumed ointment), brushes, and heated combs. She began selling her products door to door. The business grew rapidly, and Walker hired representatives throughout the United States and Latin America to peddle her system. Although she died young at the age of fifty-one, she left a multimillion-dollar estate, two-thirds of which she left to charity. A few years after Walker's death, dancer Josephine Baker, who used the treatment on her hair, introduced it to women in Paris, where it also became popular.

Thanks to the flappers and film stars who popularized the use of makeup, the cosmetics business offered new opportunities for women. Two of the most successful were Helena Rubinstein and Elizabeth Arden, who started out by selling specially designed makeup to actresses and went on to build multimillion-dollar cosmetics companies. The idea that success in business would make women less feminine was widely held, although

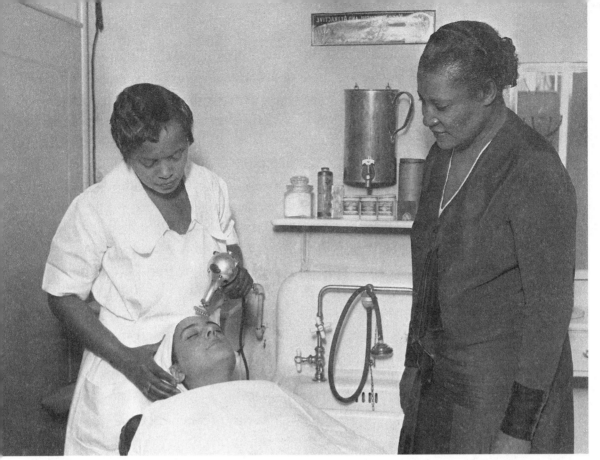

A'lelia Walker, the daughter of C.J. Walker, watches as a customer gets a facial in one of her mother's salons. C.J. Walker was one of America's early female entrepreneurs.

some women saw no contradiction between being a pretty woman and a success. As Banner notes:

> Helena Rubinstein recalled, "It was not easy being a hard-working woman in a man's world." In order to survive in the business world she became a tyrant. Her rages became legendary. She married a count, lived in lavish style, and was known as "madame." For "added courage," she wore elaborate and expensive jewel-

ry. To Rubinstein, the quest for beauty, which was central to her business and her life, did not represent enslavement, but was a "force . . . to make you feel greater than you are."[73]

Women in the Professions

The idea that a woman's proper workplace was the home was not confined to the business world. In the professions, a similar mind-set prevailed. Women found a number of careers available to them, but,

A Woman Postmaster

After widow Minnie Corum and her sons moved to Encampment, Wyoming, she was appointed postmaster, a position she held for the rest of her life. Her role was highly controversial in this small town. The following excerpt is from her autobiography, "I Licked a Stamp," published in *Second to None*, by Moynihan, Russett, and Crumpacker.

When I was told [after becoming postmaster that] I had the stubborness of a billy goat and that no one could hold out against such a determined woman whose specialty was to run the whole show I finally blew my top. "You are absolutely right," I said, "We now have a woman governor in Wyoming and Texas, my old home state has Ma Fergueson at it's [sic] helm. I am in a position to get a lot of pointers from these illustrious women for I know both of them personally."

like women in business, professional women faced roadblocks to the top jobs. Whether in law, medicine, or education, some jobs were considered women's work and others were considered only appropriate for men.

Law, in particular, was a profession that society defined as belonging to men, although women filled jobs that were vital in law offices and courtrooms. For example, women became court reporters, the people who write down every word spoken during a trial. Seldom did women become lawyers; more rarely still did women become judges. And although by 1930 the number of women lawyers had almost doubled from the number in 1920, women still made up only 2.1 percent of all lawyers.

There were, of course, exceptions—women who made their way to the top. One example was Mabel Walker Willebrandt, who earned a law degree from the University of Southern California and then set up an office with two male colleagues who were also graduates of USC. Eventually, she became a public defender and later helped found the Women Lawyers Association of Los Angeles. Finally, in 1921 she received an appointment as assistant attorney general of the United States. She attributed her rise to upper-level jobs to her careful use of every opportunity that came her way. Another example was Florence E. Allen from Cleveland, Ohio. She had earned a law degree at New York University and returned to Cleveland, where she represented suffragists in their various legal battles. In 1920 she was elected as a judge of the Court of Common Pleas; she later campaigned and was elected to the Ohio

Supreme Court and reelected in 1928. In so doing, Allen achieved the highest judicial position yet held by any woman in America.

Women in Medicine

As in the law profession, the medical profession also had what society considered men's jobs and women's jobs: The doctors were men, and the nurses were women. Nursing was the most feminized of all the professions. By the end of the decade 98 percent of nurses were women. To most men and women, nursing seemed naturally women's work. Brown notes, "As one contemporary observed, 'women had been the nurses of mankind throughout all time.'"[74]

Many nurses worked in the public health clinics for children, where they taught mothers tips for raising healthy children. In addition, they examined babies and young children and gave them whatever shots were required. Most of the nurses, however, worked in hospitals. The hospital nurse's primary role was to feed and care for patients and provide for their comfort. They had little decision-making power, however: Physicians, most of them men, managed the treatment. Nurses were seen as technicians whose job was to simply carry out doctors' orders.

Contributing to this view of nurses was an attitude that women had long endured, that higher education should be reserved for men. Brown cites a report that "concluded that nurses' training was in some instances mired in an apprenticeship 'earn-while-you-learn

Nurses tend to a road-accident victim. During the 1920s, nursing was considered women's work.

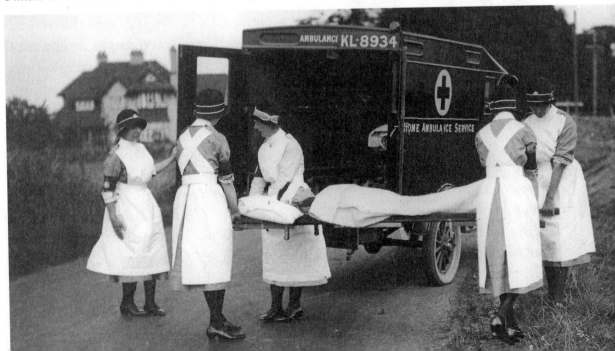

system.'"[75] In other words, nursing was something to learn by doing, not through rigorous study in a classroom or laboratory. Still, there was some effort to upgrade the educational standards of nurses during the 1920s. For example, Annie W. Goodrich of the Yale University School of Nursing recommended a college degree, two years of coursework in nursing, and clinical experience. Private physicians and hospital administrators, however, argued against her recommendations and temporarily defeated them. They said that nurses would be overtrained and too expensive to hire. Nurses suspected that doctors were afraid that well-trained nurses might interfere with their treatment plans or even suggest better ones.

Whatever its limitations, nursing as a career was clearly open to women. However, a woman who wanted to become a doctor faced many obstacles. As a result, the number of women doctors actually declined during the 1920s. In 1920 there were fifty-nine women doctors for every one thousand male doctors; by 1930 that ratio had declined to fifty-two women for every one thousand men. The reason for the decline was that starting in the early 1920s, medical schools set quotas on the number of women who would be admitted. Sometimes the quota was as low as 5 percent of the total student body. Further reducing the number of women doctors was that 90 percent of hospitals refused to take women as interns. An article in the *New York Times* on December 9, 1923, reported that women medical students in New York City launched a movement to get hospitals to open their doors to women interns. The article stated, "Women who finish their collegiate training find it difficult to obtain further experience because internships are not available to women. They are told by hospital authorities that there is a lack of quarters for women, and for that reason principally they may not be used as interns."[76] The issue of living quarters seemed to women just a ruse for preventing them from becoming doctors by denying them a chance of completing an internship. The few women who managed to overcome such obstacles and become doctors faced other problems. For example, a woman doctor in California found that some of her patients expected to be treated at half the usual rate because she was a woman.

There were a few opportunities, however, that favored women doctors. For example, women doctors, along with public health nurses, were usually hired to staff the new children's clinics, which the government had begun financing in 1921 to improve children's health and reduce the infant mortality rate. When New York City set up the Bureau of Child Hygiene to oversee clinics there,

The Need for Health Workers

On August 12, 1923, the *New York Times* reported on the number of African American women doctors, dentists, and nurses that were currently practicing and identified the number of additional ones that were needed. The article is reprinted in Janeway's *Women: Their Changing Roles.*

There are sixty-five negro women physicians, surgeons and osteopaths in this country, according to figures compiled by the Department of the Interior through Howard University. There are five negro women who practice dentistry in the United States. Other statistics show that the average yearly increase of negro physicians is sixty-three when there is need of an annual increase of at least 450. The average number of additional dentists graduating every year is sixty-three, but there should be 500. The same condition applies with regard to trained nurses, ninety being turned out each year when 600 are needed. Data collected by the university show that more negro physicians and dentists are practicing in the cities of New York, Philadelphia, Washington, Cleveland and Chicago than in the sixteen Southern States combined, where fully 8,000,000 negroes live.

Dr. Josephine Baker became its director. This was at that time the highest level position any woman doctor had ever held. In the private sector, a few women doctors found positions in department stores. The owners of these businesses wanted someone to look after the health of the sales people, many of whom were women. Researcher Frances R. Donovan notes: "The employer, in his enlightened selfishness, realizes that the health of his workers is a factor in his profits. He therefore maintains a force of doctors, nurses, dentists, and chiropodists [foot doctors] to examine them when they enter his employ and to look after them during their period of employment."[77]

Women in Education and Research

Unlike law and medicine, education was a profession that had long attracted and encouraged women. Before the 1920s, in fact, teaching had always been a major source of employment for women. During the 1920s, 57 percent of all employed women were public school teachers. They were graduates of normal schools, which were colleges offering one- or two-year programs designed to train teachers.

Most of the women teachers taught in one-room country schools or in elementary schools. Country school teachers taught all subjects to students ranging from first through eighth grade. The teacher had to organize classes in reading, writing, mathematics, science, history, and literature and tailor instruction to eight different levels. Besides the actual teaching, they were also responsible for making sure, in cold weather, that there was wood or coal for the furnace, ordering all materials, and repairing any broken equipment. Teachers in larger towns had an easier job. Usually, a teacher there had a class of students who were all in the same grade, although she was still responsible for teaching all the subjects.

As in the other professions, there were jobs that women could not usually aspire to. These generally related to administration. Country school teachers were under the supervision of a school board that was usually male dominated. In the towns, elementary schools were run by the principals, who were almost always male. Principals often had a patronizing attitude toward the teachers, keeping a watchful and protective eye on their attendance and conduct. One Minnesota teacher worked under a male principal who referred to the female teaching staff as "My girls." Contributing to such attitudes was the fact

that elementary school teachers were primarily young, single women; most would resign when they married, and most school districts would not hire married woman as teachers. As late as 1928, one-third of all school districts required women teachers to resign when they married.

At the high school level, women were treated more as men's equals. High school teachers had earned a four-year college degree and were trained in a particular academic discipline. Still, there were ways in which men and women were treated differently. Usually women taught grammar and literature, foreign languages, and occasionally history or social studies. Men, on the other hand, taught mathematics or science. Women seldom served as department leaders unless there were no men in the department, as often happened in English and language departments. Rarely did a woman serve as principal or superintendent of schools, as these also were considered men's jobs.

If women rarely found parity with their male colleagues, the situation was far more unequal for black women, who were discriminated against because of gender and race. Only in a handful of instances, such as that of Mary McLeod Bethune, did a black woman rise to become an administrator of a school. In 1904 in Daytona Beach, Florida, with supplies that cost $1.50, Bethune started teaching six children: five girls and her son Albert. By 1923 Bethune had managed to acquire a twenty-acre campus and facilities for three hundred female students—elementary and secondary students as well as would-be teachers in training. She then merged her school, called Daytona Normal and Industrial Institute, with Cookman Institute in Jacksonville, Florida. The new school, which was now coed, became the Bethune-Cookman College in 1929. Three years later it became an accredited junior college. Bethune's mission had been to help young black women gain the skills they needed to escape from domestic service and find respect as teachers. Eventually

that goal grew to helping all black students who wanted to do so to earn teaching credentials in an accredited school.

Besides the work of a school administrator, the top-level professional jobs in education were in college teaching and research. These were jobs that required advanced degrees, and women eagerly pursued the necessary education. As a result, the number of women earning doctoral degrees during the 1920s increased. Woloch notes that "women capitalized briefly on progressive gains. Since 1910, the proportion of doctorates earned by women rose—from 10 percent that year to 15.1 percent in 1920 to 15.4 percent in 1930."[78]

Bethune Builds a College

I n the following excerpt from the article "Faith That Moved a Dump Heap," Mary McLeod Bethune explains how she transformed a dump into a junior college campus to educate black women and men. Her school eventually became an accredited four-year college. The excerpt is reprinted in *Women's America: Refocusing the Past*, edited by Linda K. Kerber and Jane De Hart Mathews.

Near by was a field, popularly called Hell's Hole, which was used as a dumping ground. I approached the owner,

determined to buy it. The price was $250. In a daze, he finally agreed to take five dollars down, and the balance in two years. I promised to be back in a few days with the initial payment. He never knew it, but I didn't have five dollars. I raised this sum selling ice cream and sweet-potato pies to the workmen on construction jobs, and I took the owner his money in small change wrapped in my handkerchief.

That's how the Bethune-Cookman college campus started.

Margaret Mead visits with children on the island of Bali. During the 1920s, Mead traveled throughout the Pacific to collect data on the inhabitants of remote islands.

As was true at the secondary level, some disciplines came to be seen as more appropriate for women than for men. Women found greater acceptance both as students and later as professors in English, modern language, sociology, and psychology departments than in such departments as biology, botany, and zoology. Women doing research primarily were counseled to take on projects in agriculture, home economics, and public health, since these disciplines were thought by male college administrators to fit nicely with the domestic talents of women as providers of the basic necessities of food, clothing, and nurturing. As a result of such attitudes, women seldom had opportunities to do research in physics, chemistry, or biology.

Some women, however, turned such prejudice to their advantage, making enormous contributions in fields such as anthropology by investigating questions overlooked by their male colleagues. One such pioneer was Margaret Mead. While still a graduate student studying anthropology at Columbia University, she persuaded the administrators there to permit her to do fieldwork outside of North America. She wanted to collect data concerning the language and customs of people on remote islands in the Pacific Ocean. This being an era when even educated whites accepted the racist idea that white women were in danger of sexual assaults by black men, Mead's supervisors objected to her being alone among native tribesmen. Mead ignored such concerns and went anyway. During her field research she compiled volumes of data, which formed the basis for many books she wrote.

Mead, however, was something of an exception. Most women who wanted teaching positions at the college level depended on the goodwill of men to get hired and therefore had to follow their advice. In any case, when posting positions, many top universities simply refused to consider a woman's application, no matter what her qualifications were. If a woman was hired, she sometimes had to make humiliating concessions. For example, Alice Hamilton, who had a doctoral degree, was internationally known for her research in industrial toxicology. When she was invited to join the Harvard Medical School faculty, one of the conditions for her hiring was to agree that she would never march with her male colleagues in academic processions. In other words, she was to remain invisible to the public.

In addition, for the women who were hired for college teaching positions, the pay was poor. For example, women teaching at colleges where only women were enrolled were paid 73 percent of what men were paid. In coed institutions, the inequities were even worse: Women earned just 53 percent of what their male colleagues were paid.

Women as Librarians

Although women had to battle discrimination in college teaching, those who chose to become librarians often found jobs readily. Following World War I, government and private funds for the building of new libraries had greatly increased, so many more librarians were needed. Since librarians' salaries were low, men tended to pursue higher-paying jobs in professions from which women were excluded. Women, moreover, were considered particularly suited for librarianship, since the duties involved service in ways thought similar to their domestic roles. Historians Suzanne Hildenbrand and Judith Pryor note the attitude that accompanied the influx of women librarians in the 1920s:

> The first libraries to welcome women workers were public libraries trying to encourage more people to visit them by promoting a homelike, genteel atmosphere.... Many still thought women were suited to librarianship because of their feminine qualities—attention to detail, rapport with children, service orientation.[79]

In addition, a job in a library appealed to educated women who liked reading and who found a library a pleasant and quiet place to work with books and still earn a salary. Even in libraries, gender discrimination existed, since women were almost never hired as administrators—those who managed the budget or purchased the books.

During the 1920s, several women made important contributions that improved library services. For example, Jennie M. Flexner developed programs in adult education and counseling for adult readers. Anne Carroll Moore began children's storytelling hours, a practice that libraries throughout the country copied. The need for library services was particularly great among blacks in the South. Hildenbrand and Pryor note: "Within the constraints of segregated southern society, pioneering black women struggled to obtain libraries for blacks, to establish appropriate collections featuring black culture and history, [and] to develop professional education and standards for service to black communities."[80] In Charleston, South Carolina, a black woman named Susan Dart Butler began to meet that need for the black community by opening a library housing books from her deceased father's collection.

Combining Career and Family

During the 1920s, despite all the obstacles placed before them, women entered business or the professions in dramatically greater numbers than in the past. Many were middle-class, married women who wanted to combine a career with marriage. Woloch calls this phenomenon "a novel, modern goal."[81] Women struggled, however, trying to balance their role as homemakers against the demands of their careers. The number of women who tried to accomplish this balance increased from 19.3 percent in 1920 to 24.7 percent in 1930.

Career women made great contributions to the social and financial life of the nation during the 1920s by working in a variety of business and professional jobs. Those who struggled to find room at the upper levels of business and the professions made an additional contribution. Their work opened opportunities for women in decades to come. Thanks to the efforts of pioneers like Madame C.J. Walker and Margaret Mead, the glass ceiling, that invisible barrier that keeps qualified, talented individuals from achieving their full potential, is no longer the unbreachable barrier it once was.

Chapter 5:
Working-Class Women

Though business and professional women worked because they chose to, most of the women who worked outside the home did so out of economic need. Either their husbands earned too little to support the family adequately or, in the case of women on their own, they had to support themselves. Working-class women, like women in business and the professions, endured discrimination. Often they were simply not considered for a job if a man wanted it.

Service Jobs

For working women the most jobs were in domestic service. For decades, women had worked and lived as servants in homes of wealthier families, but by the 1920s, the practice of providing housing for servants was less common. Instead, women in domestic service lived with other single working women. Domestic servants became day laborers, although they essentially did the same chores. For example, they still did laundry, cleaning, and cooking. Living independently did not make the work any more pleasant. Flossie Cole described her return to domestic work after losing her factory job as "back to the drudge house."[82]

Domestic service jobs often were the only option for black women because racial discrimination was so widely practiced during the 1920s. In 1922 nearly 1 million African American women worked in domestic service. Many of these women had moved with their families from farms in the South in search of a better life. What they found, however, was that they were relegated to the hardest, most menial tasks. For those who got jobs as live-in servants, living conditions were poor. Social historian Elizabeth Ross Haynes summarizes the disadvantages that faced these women: "namely, basement living quarters, poor working conditions, too long hours, no Sundays off, no standards of efficiency, and the servant 'brand.'"[83]

Black women moving to cities such as Washington, D.C., experienced additional adjustments. For example, in the

The most common occupations for working women in the 1920s were in domestic service. Like this woman, many worked as maids.

South, they had worked on farms, taking orders from men; now they worked for women. Moreover, as domestic servants they were required to wear uniforms. They hated the uniforms because they symbolized the white employer's power. One woman, Ophilia Simpson, who worked as a servant in Washington, D.C., offered this opinion of uniforms:

> Them uniforms just seemed to make them know you was theirs. Some say you wore them to show different jobs you was doing. Time in grey. Other

times in black. But mostly them things just showed you was always at their beck and call. Really that's all them things means![84]

For a black woman, there often was little choice at first but to work as a live-in servant. In the Washington, D.C. area, black women banded together in penny savers clubs, organizations that provided some opportunities for socializing. If a member fell ill, fellow members would help support her until she could return to work. Most important, however, these clubs functioned as banks, setting up small savings accounts to which members contributed. After saving for about six years, a woman might accumulate enough money to make the transition from live-in servant to day work.

For an African American woman, being a day worker represented a step up from being a live-in servant. Young women enjoyed living in boardinghouses with other day workers. Although they continued to do the same jobs, just as white day laborers did, there was a sense of independence they found uplifting. Elizabeth Clark-Lewis reports how one woman perceived the difference:

> Virginia Lacey described the new experience with an employer this way: "She'd meet you at the door, tell you how she wanted her house done,

and she'd be gone. You did the work without her in the way, slowing you up. On a day job we all knew how to get everything done—but, in your own way. Having anybody around will make you work slower. . . . I'd go to whatever house I'd have to be to work at. I change to my work clothes and then clean the house. . . . Wearing your own clothes—that's like you being your own boss! You was on your own job for a day and pay, then go home."[85]

There were also social advantages to day work. Women paid by the day could put in a six-day week and attend church on Sunday if they wanted to. Having that choice enhanced the feeling of independence.

In addition to domestic work, other kinds of service jobs were available to women. One of the big changes was the establishment of power laundries, which laundered linens for hotels and restaurants or did wet-wash or rough-dry loads for families. In power laundries, while men operated the machines and lifted heavy loads, women marked the items in the loads so they could be returned to the proper customer. They also shook out wet laundry and did the ironing. Jobs in laundries offered some variety and were not physically hard, but women's pay was low, and the atmosphere was damp and often hot.

A large number of women, both black and white, found somewhat more pleasant conditions working as elevator operators. In the 1920s elevators were not self-serve: Each one had an operator, who listened to the requests for floors as passengers got on. When the elevator was loaded, she operated the lever—which resembled a short-handled crank—that sent the elevator's car up or down. Although elevator operators were paid low wages and the work was monotonous, the hardest part of the job was standing in one spot for several hours at a time.

Jobs in Agriculture

Although many women found work in the cities, during the 1920s women also worked on farms, especially in the rural South. Since many of the farms were small subsistence operations, these women performed a variety of chores while their husbands either worked elsewhere on the farm or as laborers in mines or factories. These farm women worked fields and planted crops, tended to farm animals, and harvested in the fall. All of these tasks required hard physical work and long hours, but the women derived satisfaction knowing that they were working for themselves and their families. For example, Stephanie Kosior, who helped her husband on their family tobacco farm, did all the cooking and baking on a wood stove in a kitchen without hot, running water. During harvest, she helped with the work by hanging the tobacco leaves on racks to dry. She describes the exhaustion she felt one evening after spending the day hanging the leaves up:

All I remember doing is getting home, coming in here from the fields and I just sprawled out on the floor. Sometimes I think . . . I got a little sunstroke. I was panting. I couldn't get my breath for half an hour. So everybody was still out there, I had to come in earlier to start the supper. But I do remember that. Just sprawling, laying, stretching right out on the floor. And I thought, "I'll never get my breath back." The heat, everything. You know, when you're harvesting, it's August . . . oh, that is hot! It isn't so much the work, but it's the heat.[86]

Not all farms in the South, however, were small operations. Large cotton and peanut plantations required large numbers of laborers. African American women, with no other opportunities for work, took jobs on these plantations. For example, a white woman who owned over a thousand acres of land in Alabama hired black women to do whatever needed to be done. She said, "Down here women do almost any kind of work on the farm from handling a two-horse plow, and hoeing and pulling fodder, to clearing new ground."[87] On peanut farms, women pulled up peanut bushes by hand and put them up to dry. When the plants were dry, they took them to a steam peanut-picker, which removed the peanuts. They then shoveled the peanuts into sacks. As was often the case on farms, all of the work was done outdoors, regardless of the weather, since the crop had to be harvested as soon as it was ripe.

Factory Jobs

Less physically demanding than farmwork were the many kinds of factory jobs that were available to women. Women worked in factories producing processed foods, clothing, shoes, and tobacco products. Most factories by the 1920s had streamlined and mechanized production, so a worker operated a machine that did one task over and over. A worker stayed in one spot repeating the same task for her entire shift, which sometimes was as long as ten hours. For example, in a candy factory, a woman might operate the machine that squirted a premeasured amount of chocolate coating to cover a piece of candy. The worst part of such a job was the monotony.

In textile mills and clothing factories, workers similarly operated machines that performed one step in a larger process. The manufacture of rayon, or artificial silk, was typical of the textile industry. In

A black family hoes rows of cotton on a plantation in Alabama. Many African American women in the South performed backbreaking labor on white-owned plantations.

rayon factories, men worked the machines that extracted cellulose from fiber and wove it into rayon thread. Women then reeled the thread into skeins and inspected the thread for flaws. Women also operated the looms, which wove the rayon thread into bolts of cloth, and knitting machines, which produced articles of clothing. Because making rayon was a chemical process, workers in these factories breathed polluted air, and many had rashes and other skin problems from exposure to the harsh chemicals. Added to this foul atmosphere was the heat, since many textile factories were located in the South.

The manufacture of tobacco products was also transformed in the 1920s. Prior to that time, tobacco leaves were rolled into cigars by hand; in the 1920s,

machines rolled not just cigars but cigarettes as well. Cigarettes were manufactured using several separate machines, one each for cutting, drying, and shredding the tobacco, and another for rolling the cigarettes. Again, a woman stood beside one machine repeating the same task over and over. Tobacco factories, usually located in the South, were often hot, and the air was dusty and filled with tobacco odors. These conditions made the job both unpleasant and unhealthful.

Factory Work for Black Women

Black women also worked in factories, mostly making cigars or cigarettes, but others held jobs in textile mills, nut- and crab-packing plants, and slaughter and

Young African American women roll cigars, one of the factory jobs available to black women in the 1920s.

meatpacking houses. Almost always, black women were given the least desirable jobs. For example, while white women operated the machines in textile mills, black women scrubbed the floors and cleaned lint from the machines. In nut-packing plants, black women worked to move heavy bags loaded with nuts to the packaging machines, which white women operated.

In tobacco factories, black women had to sit on hard floors while they stripped leaves from the stalks. In slaughtering houses, they worked on the stockyard floor, cleaning spattered blood and dragging bags filled with unusable animal parts to the waste depository. In the crab factories in Maryland and Virginia, black women sat on boxes and cleaned crabs that had been steamed and cooled. They cracked the shell and removed the usable meat, which they sorted between white and dark. This task they repeated all day every day, working in damp cement buildings. Some women worked in jobs such as these for twenty or thirty years with no hope of a pension when they retired.

Because of racial attitudes during the 1920s, black women suffered from conditions that white women never had to face. In some places, for example, black women had to walk long distances from their homes if blacks were not allowed to live in the neighborhoods close to their workplaces. Once at work, many black women had to deal with terrible conditions. The worst places did not even have toilets. Because none of these factories had air filters or temperature control, the women often breathed unhealthy air and suffered from stifling heat during the warm months.

On rare occasions black women were hired to do the same tasks as white women. A very few black women became typists, for example. Others got jobs operating machines in furniture and shoe factories and at printing establishments. A few had semiskilled jobs assembling products in electric supply, paper box, rubber, and textile factories. In each case, however, the black women were paid the lowest wages, and they were the first to be fired when the workforce was reduced or when white women were available for hire.

Striking for Better Conditions

In some areas of the country, women tried to solve the problems of low wages and poor working conditions by striking. The garment and mill workers in Massachusetts and New York were the first to unionize, and the women working in those industries in the South soon followed. One of the many strikes that occurred in the South was the work stoppage at the rayon plant in Elizabethton, Tennessee, where women objected to low pay, long hours, and controlling rules. Historian Jacquelyn Dowd Hall describes their complaints about the rules:

Women in particular were singled out for petty regulations, aimed not just at extracting labor but at shaping deportment as well. They were forbidden to wear makeup; in some departments they were required to purchase uniforms. Most galling of all was company surveillance of the washroom. According to Bessie Edens, who was promoted to "forelady" in the twisting room, "men could do what they wanted to in their own department," but women had to get a pass to leave the shop floor. "If we went to the bathroom they'd follow us."[88]

Leaders of the Elizabethton strike were militant and willing to advocate violence. Eventually, the National Guard was called in to control the strikers. In the end, the strike was defeated, and the union leaders lost their jobs. This pattern was repeated as employers across the South used an array of tactics, such as firing and spying, to defeat strikes and prevent women from organizing to gain improved working conditions and wages. Historians note that the movement of women during the 1920s to unionize had failed to stop their exploitation. Nancy Cott and Elizabeth Pleck conclude that strikes had succeeded in "releasing some women from some of the misery of toil, but simultaneously confirming their place in those jobs most conducive to exploitation."[89]

Metal Trades and Electric Supply Industries

There were a few bright spots for working women. For example, manpower shortages caused by World War I opened jobs to women in industries that had been previously all-male. These were the metal trades and electric supply industries. In iron and steel foundries, women operated machines that poured heated liquid metal into forms that shaped parts for larger machines. In steel mills, they fed sheets of metal into presses that made small metal parts. Women also varnished and lacquered these parts, and wrapped, packaged, and labeled the finished products. A 1927 survey found that 526 women worked as metal polishers and grinders and 127 were welders. Author Sophonisba P. Breckinridge comments:

These women were interviewed and most of them made favorable comments regarding their work. It was "interesting," it paid well and, according to a number, in spite of metal dust or danger from sparks, it was "easier" work than that previously done in domestic service or work in a cotton mill, a silk mill or a garment factory.[90]

In addition, women worked in needle and pin factories and also contributed to making jewelry, typewriters, screws, and hardware. In all of the metal factories, women stood on their feet in one spot by one machine for many hours. Some worked in dangerous conditions in which they breathed air filled with metal dust. Since protective glasses were not available, women risked eye injuries from flying metal shavings.

The electrical components industry was one in which women actually were valued employees. They wound and insulated electrical coils by hand or machine, they operated punch and drill presses, and they inspected and tested motors to make sure they worked properly. Women manufactured electric light bulbs, winding and mounting the filaments and attaching the glass globe to the base. At the time it was thought that women had greater finger dexterity than men, and so were more suited for intricate tasks. Breckinridge notes, "Women are especially fitted for this work because, according to one employer's statement, 'Lamp making is too delicate work to be done economically by men.'"[91] Women also worked making radios, a task that involved at least nineteen different operations. One of the operations, for example, was connecting wires with a light handheld soldering iron, a process a worker repeated over and over during the course of the workday. Such repetitious work was hardly fulfilling. One woman who did this monotonous task commented, "Soldering hundreds and over a thousand little wires a day made me crazy."[92]

A young woman assembles telephones. Some women considered this type of work to be easier than domestic service or factory work.

Office Jobs

Though some women who worked in offices had jobs identified as business careers, most of the women in offices held jobs that required no more skill than those found in factories. Filing documents was one such job. Besides working as file clerks, women operated machines such as typewriters, dictation machines, and adding machines. Operating these devices was no more complicated and required no more education than operating a machine in a factory. Women, however, liked office jobs better than those in factories because operating a machine in an office had higher

The Elizabethton Strike

❦

In "'Disorderly Women' and Labor Militancy in the Appalachian South, 1920s," Jacquelyn Dowd Hall tells how the Elizabethton strike began in the rayon plant. Before it ended six weeks later with no gains for the workers, the conflict had escalated into a violent confrontation between the troopers and the strikers. Hall's essay is reprinted in *Major Problems in American Women's History*, edited by Mary Beth Norton and Ruth M. Alexander.

The machines whirred, and work began as usual. But the reeling room stirred with anticipation. The day before, March 12, 1929, all but seventeen of the 360 women in the inspection room next door had walked out in protest against low wages, petty rules, and high-handed attitudes. Now they were gathered at the factory gate, refusing to work but ready to negotiate. When 9:00 A.M. approached and the plant manager failed to appear, they broke past the guards and rushed through the plant, urging their co-workers out on strike. By 1:40 P.M. the machines were idle and the plant was closed.

The Elizabethton conflict rocked Carter County and made national headlines. Before March ended, the spirit of protest had jumbled the Blue Ridge and spread through the Piedmont. Gastonia, Marion, and Danville saw the most bitter conflicts, but dozens of towns were shocked by an unexpected workers' revolt.

status than the "manual" labor of domestic or factory work. Though working women thought office jobs held higher prestige, the wages were no better than wages in factories.

Discrimination and Bad Conditions

All women, black and white, experienced discrimination when it came to pay, regardless of the workplace or the task involved. Male employers felt that paying women less than men, even for the same work, was justified. Managers widely assumed that women who worked were only doing so temporarily as a way of keeping busy before they settled into marriage. If women worked after they married, it was assumed they were only trying to earn "pin money"—that is,

Women of the Roaring Twenties

money for minor purchases—while their husbands were the ones actually supporting the family. Author Susan Householder Van Horn notes

> Society considered that women's pay was 'pin money' to be used for small and unimportant luxuries. The implication was that women were working to keep idleness at bay and to indulge their small whims. The husband still remained the family breadwinner; bread was more important than pins.[93]

Even when women worked in jobs that men refused to do, however, they still received low wages.

Although it was sometimes true that a woman's earnings were not crucial to the family's survival, that was beside the point, since such wage discrimination tended to send the wrong message to women. Brown explains:

> What women's [lower] wages signaled to women was their inferiority outside the confines of the home, the need for male protection, and the realization that independence and mobility were not seen as goals appropriate for them. The ultimate effect of low wages for women was to reinforce "docility, the perverse sense of marginality, that kept most women immobile, poverty-wage workers."[94]

Working women, despite the low value placed on their services, contributed greatly to the economic growth of the United States during the 1920s. The economic success of the decade depended in large part on their willingness to endure long hours and poor working conditions and low pay. Because they had little power and money to fight discrimination, working women needed help from outside their own ranks. That help came from some of the women political activists who took it upon themselves to pressure the nation's leaders to ease the burdens on working women.

Chapter 6:
Political Activists

August 26, 1920, marks the day American women gained the right to vote. Expectations ran high that the newly acquired power of the ballot box would bring needed improvements to women's lives. But during the decade, the anticipated power never materialized, and hopes for change were dashed. In part this was due to a rising conservative attitude in the nation that quelled the spirit for reform. Furthermore, women themselves were distracted from taking up the causes their mothers and grandmothers had pursued. Historian Judith Papachristou notes: "There was more to buy, more money with which to buy it, and a beguiling new advertising industry, all of which turned the housewife into a purchasing agent and made shopping a time-consuming and complicated activity."[95] Moreover, the women who had been unified by their efforts to obtain the vote found themselves at odds over other issues in as little as six months after they had achieved their voting right.

Nevertheless, the 1920s was a decade rich in women's political activities. Many new leagues and organizations formed around various issues. The women in these new organizations worked for causes as diverse as promoting women's and children's health, ending the lynching of blacks, Prohibition, and peace. The major issue among political activists, however, centered on whether women should be protected or be independent and equal with men.

Women Organize

Women formed many new organizations with the belief that collective action was the only way to bring results. Women who had been united in the National American Women Suffrage Association (NAWSA) disbanded that organization once they had enfranchised 26 million American women. Political activist Carrie Chapman Catt presided over the last NAWSA convention and helped to found its successor, the National League of Women Voters (NLWV). This new organization set as its goals to educate the electorate, to open participation in political parties to women, and to support laws to protect women and children. Soon after the NLWV was formed, militant feminists formed their own organization and challenged the fledgling league. In 1921 Alice Paul led eight thousand women in the formation of the National Woman's Party (NWP). These women were determined to achieve political equality for women. Their intent, then, was to support women candidates, the goal being that half of all elected officials would be women.

While these two organizations dominated the political discussion and activity during the 1920s, several other organizations were formed to advance specific causes. For example, Lida Hafford formed the General Federation of Women's Clubs (GFWC), gaining 2.8 million members, to improve social conditions for women and children. Florence Kelley organized forty thousand women into the National Consumers' League (NCL) to establish a minimum-wage scale for women. Margaret Robin organized the Women's Trade Union League (WTUL) to help women form their own unions. Jewish women banded together into the National Council of Jewish Women (NCJW) to address the concerns of immigrants, many of whom were Jewish; Catholic women, meanwhile, banded together into the National Council of Catholic Women (NCCW) to improve

A large crowd turns out for a 1921 Women's Freedom League rally. Throughout the decade, women established a number of new activist organizations.

conditions for working-class women, many of whom were Catholic.

Politically active women could see that organizations were headed in all directions, with some organizations overlapping in their goals and others competing. Leaders then developed the Women's Joint Congressional Committee (WJCC) to coordinate the activities of various women's groups and form a clearinghouse for legislation women wanted passed in Congress. Maud Wood Park of the NLWV chaired this organization, and Florence V. Watkins of the National Congress of Mothers (NCM) became its first secretary. The plan was to settle on a particular bill and then find a sympathetic member of Congress who would introduce it, either in the House of Representatives or the Senate. Members of the WJCC, for their part, would lobby other congressmen to vote for the bill in question. This group had on its agenda the six P's, legislation in six areas all beginning with the letter "p": Prohibition, public schools, protection of infants (its top priority), physical education in public schools, peace through arms reduction, and protection of women in industry. This organization, which did a good job tracking progress of bills in Congress, became a powerful lobby in Washington, D.C. Part of its power derived from male politicians'

fear that women in a particular district would vote as a bloc.

The First Health Care Bill

As it turned out, women rarely voted as a bloc. Still, women were widely in agreement that steps needed to be taken to promote women's and children's health. In the early 1920s, America ranked eleventh out of twenty industrialized nations in infant mortality and seventeenth in maternal mortality. This meant that 200,000 infants and eighteen thousand mothers were dying annually. Leaders of women's organizations visited Senator Morris Sheppard of Texas and Iowa congressman Horace Towner and persuaded them to introduce a bill to improve the health of infants and mothers. President Warren G. Harding endorsed it as well. The bill had the support of the American Federation of Labor, the National Catholic Welfare Conference, and women doctors such as Dr. Josephine Baker, who declared:

> Well-baby clinics . . . should be as free as the public schools, in either case the reservation being left to the parents to take their babies or children to private schools or private physicians. . . . Public health is not a special privilege but a birthright. . . . The infant welfare station is as much a part of the public

function as the public baths, public playgrounds, libraries and schools.[96]

Of all the groups supporting the bill, the Women's Joint Congressional Committee was the most powerful because it deluged congressmen with letters. Thanks to such determined promotion, the Sheppard-Towner Act passed in July 1921.

The Sheppard-Towner Act was the first major federal welfare law. It earmarked $5,000 to every state—and an additional $5,000 if the state matched the federal funds—to provide a wide variety of services for women and children. Administration of the funds was in the hands of the Children's Bureau, which was headed by Grace Abbott. Because urban areas already had services for women and children, the Sheppard-Towner Act mostly targeted rural areas. At the end of five years, all but three states had programs. The programs operated out of centers where expectant mothers received advice, and mothers got preventive health checkups for themselves and for their babies until one year old. Public health nurses visited mothers and children in their homes, and women physicians staffed the centers. Woloch describes the centers' success: "Sheppard-Towner centers provided a great barrage of classes, literature, and health services, and reached thousands of pregnant women and millions of infants and children."[97]

The Sheppard-Towner Program Closed

In spite of the Sheppard-Towner program's success, even some women opposed it, either for what it did or what it failed to do. For example, Alice Paul of the National Woman's Party gave speeches denouncing the program because it made a blanket classification of women as mothers, when indeed many women were not. Margaret Sanger and her fellow birth-control advocates spoke out against the centers because they did not offer birth-control advice; they argued that the program encouraged women to have more children, when many of them wanted fewer. The severest opposition, however, came from the American Medical Association (AMA). Doctors deluged the AMA's professional journal with complaints that outsiders were interfering in their practice of medicine. Some historians see a monetary motive in the doctors' opposition to the Sheppard-Towner centers. According to this line of thinking, doctors saw a potentially lucrative business in giving regular checkups to pregnant mothers and infants. Whatever their motives, doctors lobbied members of Congress to end funding for the centers. The pressure worked. After funding the program from 1921 to 1929, Congress terminated it. The program did, however, have a lasting impact in that preventive health care had become a part of modern medical practice.

The First Equal Rights Amendment

In the minds of many activists, even more than access to health care, the key to well-being for women lay in gaining legal recognition of their equality with men. With this goal in mind, in 1923 the National Woman's Party proposed an Equal Rights Amendment (ERA) to the Constitution. The proposed amendment stated that "Men and women shall have equal rights throughout the United States and every place subject to its jurisdiction."[98] Woloch explains that the NWP contended that

> Women were still subordinate to men in all aspects of life, indeed over 1,000 state laws discriminated against women. The ERA would erase sex as a legal classification and make women equal in every arena, from property rights to divorce rights to employment opportunities. It would also, however, invalidate the barrage of protective laws for which women reformers had long campaigned.[99]

This proposal launched the debate over whether protective laws helped or hindered women. Alice Paul gave speeches, wrote articles, and met with congressmen, always trying to convey a single message: that protective laws that assumed that women are weak and need protection should be replaced with the ERA, which would let women compete equally on their own strengths. Leaders of other women's organizations contended that the reality of discrimination against women meant that they needed to be protected by specific laws. As Papachristou says, the debate took place "before legislative committees, in popular magazines, at political conventions, and at every important gathering of organized women."[100]

The protective laws that had been enacted over the previous decade or more covered various working conditions faced by women. The most controversial rules were several: One set a minimum wage for women; another limited a workday to no more than eight or nine hours; a third prohibited assigning women to work at night; yet another set prohibitions on women lifting heavy weights; and finally a rule prohibited work just before or just after childbirth. Protective laws actually prohibited hiring women for some jobs, such as work in mines, bowling alleys, and poolrooms, which were considered inappropriate places for women to work. Another protective law outlawed women's taking any job detrimental to health, morals, or the capacity for childbearing. All of these laws had been passed in the hope that they would protect women from exploitation.

In 1923 members of the League of Women Voters pose with an enormous roll of signatures in support of laws protecting women and children. They intend to present their petition to President Coolidge.

Independence or Protection?

The National Woman's Party strongly opposed these laws. The members objected to the labeling of women as a special class, that is, mothers or potential mothers. They also objected to improving working conditions only for women, arguing that any improvements should apply to workers as a class, not to gender. Activist Harriot Stanton Blatch said that her objection to special legislation was "not on the grounds that no protection is necessary, but because partial laws have not protected men and have thrown women out of employment or crowded them into lower grades of work."[101] Blatch pointed out that working men were also the victims of poor conditions. She said that welfare workers "always seem to think of industrial women as spavined [old and decrepit], broken-backed creatures, and the sons of Adam as tireless, self-reliant unionized supermen. Neither estimate is correct. Both need the protective aegis [oversight] of the state."[102]

The NWP preferred to provide women with the power to negotiate directly with employers regarding hours and wages. That way, the thinking ran, women could avoid losing their jobs to

Women Are Not Children

Crystal Eastman, one of the founders of the National Woman's Party, supported freedom and independence for women. In this excerpt from her essay "Equality or Protection," she quotes a Connecticut law and belittles the motives behind it. Her essay is reprinted in *Crystal Eastman on Women and Revolution*, edited by Blanche Wiesen Cook.

"No public restaurant, café, dining-room, barber shop, hair-dressing or manicuring establishment or photograph gallery shall employ any minor under sixteen years of age or any women, between the hours of 10 o'clock in the evening and 6 o'clock in the morning."

For a woman engaged in these pursuits there may be as much insult and injury in such a law as there was for all women in the pre-suffrage classification of minors, idiots [the now-outmoded term for individuals with mental retardation], criminals and women as persons denied a voice in democratic government.... It is quite usual to prohibit night work for women in advanced industrial countries.... Yet it is not maintained that women's lungs are more susceptible to the night air than the lungs of men, or that women's eyes are more injuriously affected by artificial light than the eyes of men. If this were true, we must begin by legislating against the full work-basket which the working-class mother takes up by lamp-light after her children are asleep and the dishes of the last meal are washed and put away.

No, the implication of such laws is really a moral one—women must not be allowed to work after dark lest they succumb to the dangers of the midnight streets. Although it must be obvious that in the agitation preceding the enactment of such laws the zeal of the reformers would be second to the zeal of the highly paid night-workers who are anxious to hold their trade against an invasion of skilled women.

To this sort of interference with her working life the modern woman can have but one attitude: *I am not a child. I will have none of your protection.*

men, who were not subject to minimum wages, restricted hours, and limitations on night work. NWP member Mary A. Murray said that when night work is considered, "adult women should have the same rights as adult men to engage in it if they so choose. It is for them and not for others to decide if their earnings will compensate for changing night to day."[103]

Members of the National League of Women Voters supported protective laws with equally strong arguments and strong words. They gave speeches at political gatherings and women's conferences and sent editorials to magazines and newspapers. Mary Anderson, director of the Women's Bureau, said that the militants had "a kind of hysterical feminism with a slogan for a program," and Florence Kelley said the ERA was a "slogan of the insane."[104] They argued that because women were different from men and because motherhood placed women at a permanent disadvantage in the workplace, they would always need protective laws. "'Women cannot be made men' by constitutional amendment," Kelley argued, "and thus required laws 'different than those needed by men.'"[105]

League members also argued that it was ludicrous to think that women could bargain for themselves. Perhaps professional and business career women could bargain with employers for salary, the NLWV argued, but women industrial workers had no power to do so. The league members thought that the NWP seemed to favor the rights of the few over the needs of the many. As one league member said, "Just as robber barons placed profit before health, income before safety, and property before welfare, so the NWP elevated its demands."[106] Those in favor of the laws pointed out that protective laws greatly helped workers in women's occupations, such as nursing and office work; however, they admitted that a minority of women working in what were considered men's jobs, such as printing and metalwork, might find their wages cut or their jobs eliminated when employers applied protective laws.

Advocates for the ERA were particularly single-minded, sometimes refusing to consider other issues. For example, Alice Paul of the NWP insisted that the issue of legal discrimination against women must take priority over other causes. She brushed aside the arguments of those who favored protective laws for women. Moreover, she abandoned the issue of black women's voting rights, which had originally been part of the ERA, when it appeared that white southerners would only support the amendment without it. Even fellow NWP members criticized Paul's control of the party. Crystal Eastman called her approach "a very efficient steamroller"; Freda Kirchwey called it a "tank" and a "machine"; and Bell Case La Follette said Paul was "utterly single-minded."[107] In the end, however, despite the speeches and strong words by women on each side, the ERA failed to gain the congressional votes necessary for it to be passed and sent to the states for ratification.

In 1917 Margaret Sanger is swarmed by supporters outside a New York courthouse after standing trial for dispensing contraception advice.

The Campaign for Birth Control

Meanwhile, politically active women were working on other causes. Margaret Sanger, for example, led the campaign for birth control. Sanger became convinced as early as 1916 of the need for birth control. As a nurse, she had visited a New York woman named Mrs. Sacks who had three children under five and had attempted an abortion on herself when she discovered that she was pregnant again. Sanger was present when Mrs. Sacks, who was very ill from an infection caused by the attempted abortion, pleaded with the doctor who attended her to explain how to prevent another pregnancy. When the doctor told her to tell her husband to sleep on the roof, Sanger was shocked that the only alternative to repeated pregnancies was for a woman to deprive herself of sexual gratification.

From that moment on, Sanger campaigned for birth control by setting up clinics that provided contraception advice, even though doing so was illegal. Sanger was imprisoned eight times, and each time she gained more publicity for her cause. In 1921 she and other middle-class women organized the American Birth Control League to campaign for repeal of the Comstock Act, which prohibited dispensing of contraceptives or advice. In addition, she wrote a family-limitation manual, which was also illegal because of the information it contained. In it Sanger advised women to pressure their doctors to provide information and contraceptives. Woloch says: "Margaret Sanger had taken direct action to liberate working-class women from 'enforced motherhood.' During the 1920s, she embodied and proclaimed the new ideal of sexual emancipation, just as it reached a nationwide, middle-class audience."[108]

By 1930, most women's groups had endorsed Sanger's cause, and clinics were no longer being raided by the police, as authorities decided that such facilities were providing a necessary service.

Maiden Names

In addition to campaigning for the right to contraception, politically active women campaigned for the right to retain their maiden names. The chief advocate for this cause was Ruth Hale, who had been barred from obtaining a passport unless she used her married name. She and a few of her like-minded friends formed the Lucy Stone League, named after a nineteenth-century woman who had kept her maiden name throughout her life. Hale, who was quoted in an article in the *New York Times*, pointed out that her organization saw no reason to treat men and women differently on this one issue: "This league was organized to protect women who desire to keep their own names and identity after marriage. All the laws now in force apply equally to men and women and it was only social custom which compelled women to adopt the names of their husbands."[109] The women in the Lucy Stone League pressured the government to make the use of maiden names legal by writing editorials, holding rallies, and lobbying.

The league was successful in its efforts. When Ruth Hale and her husband, Haywood Brown, bought a house, she wanted her maiden name on the deed. When pressed to sign as Mrs. Haywood Brown, Hale declined and said that purchasing a house did not require her to lose her individuality. The real estate representatives came to her aid, and the deed was drawn up to read, "Haywood Brown and Ruth Hale, his wife."[110] This issue was more of a symbol of women's rights than an urgent need for change. Crystal Eastman said,

Symbols are vastly important, and certainly this taking your husband's name is one of the most devastating symbols of "subjection" that remain. And yet I don't think keeping your own name is the ultimate test of a Feminist. I don't feel like walking out of a woman's house because she has not done it.[111]

Other Causes

Politically active women also worked on other causes, though they drew less attention than health care, equal rights, and birth control. One such cause was world peace. World War I had produced millions of casualties, and women sought to prevent a repeat of that devastating conflict. Carrie Chapman Catt, who years earlier had campaigned successfully for woman suffrage, formed the National Committee on the Cause and Cure of War, whose members urged disarmament as a way to peace. Like other women activists, the members of this organization gave speeches and wrote letters to congressmen and to newspapers, promoting world peace. These activists were opposed by groups such as the National Patriotic Council and the Daughters of the American Revolution, which urged the government to boost military preparedness. Catt and her fellow activists would often stage rallies and picket outside meetings of these organizations.

Another issue over which women disagreed among themselves was Prohibition, the main cause of the Women's Christian Temperance Union (WCTU), led by Ella Boole. Prohibition had been in effect since the passage of the Eighteenth Amendment in 1918, which prohibited the manufacture, sale, and transportation of intoxicating liquor. Prohibition failed to stop the consumption of alcohol and instead gave rise to bootlegging, gang wars, police corruption, and speakeasies.

From the early 1920s, opponents worked for repeal of the amendment, but the WCTU worked to retain it by protesting in public places and distributing pamphlets on the evils of drink. WCTU members also worked with young people in a program to promote total abstinence from alcohol. As resistance to the amendment grew, some WCTU members grew tired of what they saw as a losing cause. One member noted, "This isn't the organization it used to be. It isn't popular you know. The public thinks of us—let's face it—as a bunch of old women, as frowzy fanatics. I've been viewed as queer, as an old fogey, for belonging to the WCTU."[112] The Twenty-first Amendment, passed in 1933, finally repealed Prohibition.

A woman puts a sign on the rear of her car to show her support for repealing the Eighteenth Amendment, which banned the manufacture and sale of liquor.

Though women were divided on many political and social issues, on one issue—prison reform—women were united. Mabel Walker Willebrandt began to work on prison reform in 1923 with the help of women's organizations. The need for action was apparent. Women's prisons were crowded and conditions were poor. Meals were sparse and unappetizing, quarters were infrequently cleaned, and women sat idle because there was no opportunity to work or learn new skills. Willebrandt wanted to set up a prison to serve as a model for humane treatment that could be replicated elsewhere. By 1927, Willebrandt and her fellow activists had persuaded Congress to provide land and buildings for a prison where women would be treated with dignity. The prison, located in Alderson, West Virginia, had cottages that resembled homes, and women had a voice in the management of them. The tables in the central dining room even had tablecloths. During the day women attended classes and received training in marketable skills. The success of Willebrandt's project drew attention to her cause and helped bring reforms to other prison systems.

Black Women Activists

One issue that divided women was race. Women activists in the African American community and in the white community often worked together, but black women would find their hopes for racial equality ignored if white activists felt that was necessary. On two occasions, before the Nineteenth Amendment was passed and during the struggle to pass the Equal Rights Amendment, black activists found themselves pushed to the margins of the fight for equality.

While campaigning was still going on to pass an amendment giving women the right to vote, two black activists, Ida Wells-Barnett and Adella Hunt Logan, worked alongside their white counterparts. Both women published articles making the same points that white activists made—that all women were entitled to justice and equality. When it became clear, however, that supporting the right of black women to vote threatened passage of the Nineteenth Amendment, white activists abandoned their African American colleagues. Keetley and Pettegrew explain what happened when Ida Wells-Barnett tried to join a parade in Washington, D.C., in support of woman suffrage:

She [Wells-Barnett] was told that white southern women would not agree to march in an integrated line and that she must walk with the other women of color. Wells-Barnett refused to be deprived of her rightful place and slipped in with the Chicago paraders from the sidewalk as they passed her by.[113]

After this incident, white activists continued to reject the participation of blacks in the suffrage movement. In the form that finally was adopted, the Nineteenth Amendment gave women the right to vote, but made no specific mention of the rights of black women. White southerners continued to be free to use fear and manipulation to keep black women—and men—from the voting booth.

Black Women Again Work for Suffrage

African American women made another attempt to achieve official recognition of their voting rights when women were campaigning for the Equal Rights Amendment. They wanted a clause inserted that stipulated that black women had the right to vote. Addie Hunton, field secretary of the National Association of Colored Women (NACW), organized a delegation

Black Women Need to Fight

In her 1922 essay, "The Negro Woman in Politics," Mrs. Robert M. Patterson, who had been a Socialist candidate for the Pennsylvania General Assembly, expresses her displeasure with the political ineffectiveness of black men, who, she thought, fought too meekly for their rights. In this excerpt, she calls on black women to step into the fight. The article is reprinted in *Public Women, Public Words*, edited by Dawn Keetley and John Pettegrew.

We should agitate and insist that a larger number of our young women be allowed to qualify as social workers, inspectors and investigators in welfare work, etc.; we should set our faces against the vile and insidious propaganda of separate schools. We must not permit the fight for equal civil rights to cease until it will be possible for every citizen, without regard to race, to have complete civil rights guaranteed to him or her. We should insist that there should be an extended education for all, compulsory education for youth. We should insist upon a system of education where our youths will have every advantage and opportunity to bring out the finer qualities in them. Oh! Where are you women of courage? Step out into the battle. Those of you who want the best things in life for all humankind—you who yearn for that social justice without which the advent of the brotherhood of man is a myth—step out! . . . Vote for Socialism!

of black women from fourteen states to ask leaders of the National Woman's Party to keep enfranchisement of black women as a goal. The president of the NWP refused and gave two reasons: first, that discrimination was a race issue, not a gender issue, and second, that black women should fight for the rights of black women. Keetley and Pettegrew explain the NWP's position, drawing information from two NWP articles, one by Sue White and one by Ella Rush Murray:

White says, "the Woman's Party, as an organization, is concerned only with discrimination on account of sex, and they [the African American delegates] were understood as asking us to protect them against discrimination on account of race." It was only the minority of voices in the NWP who recognized that discrimination against African American women was discrimination against *women*. The second attitude, illustrated in Murray's article, is that African American women should fight their own battles. Increasingly in the twentieth century, due to the indifference of white women, that is exactly what African American women have done.[114]

With their pleas on the issue of voting rejected, black activists debated whether they should act by themselves or continue to work with their white counterparts. The most radical of the black women leaders was Amy Jacques Garvey. She organized 2 million women members of the United Negro Improvement Association (UNIA), calling on them to work on their own behalf, rather than waiting for help from white women or anyone else. Sara L. Fernandis, however, led black women in the Cooperative Women's League of Baltimore (CWLB) in the opposite direction. Fernandis argued that it was necessary to work with groups of white activists and profit from their power. By this time, however, controversial issues such as the right to vote were no longer an issue for whites.

The Antilynching Crusade

When black women realized that they would get no help from white women with suffrage, they focused on the issue of lynching, which had long plagued blacks in the South. White supremacists had been waging what amounted to a reign of terror in an effort to intimidate blacks. For example, mobs of white men would capture, torture, and then execute a black man, usually by hanging. Usually the murderers justified their actions by claiming that the victim had committed some sort of crime. The underlying purpose of lynching, however, was to instill fear in blacks and keep them from asserting their rights.

Black women planned a number of strategies to get a bill passed specifically banning lynching. Such a bill was introduced by Congressman Leonidas C. Dyer of Missouri, and in 1922 the Northeastern Federation of Colored Women's Clubs had a delegation ready to meet with the highly influential Senator Henry Cabot Lodge of Massachussetts to urge him to vote for the bill. The Alpha Kappa Alpha sorority, an organization of black college-educated women, sent a telegram to President Warren G. Harding urging him to support Dyer's bill. The National Association of Colored Women formed delegations assigned to contact states' congressmen whose support was needed for passage. Three influential black women leaders—antilynching crusader Ida B. Wells-Barnett, NACW president Hallie Q. Brown, and Rhode Island suffragist Mary B. Jackson—met with President Harding and asked him to support the Dyer bill. Mary B. Talbert, one of the founders of the NAACP, carried on the most extensive campaign in support of the bill. She organized an executive committee of fifteen women who supervised seven hundred workers in states around the nation in the antilynching crusade. Rosalyn Terborg-Penn elaborates on her strategy:

Her aim was to "unite a million women to stop lynching," by arousing the consciences of both black and white women. One of Talbert's strategies was to provide statistics that showed that victims of lynching were not what propagandists called sex-hungry black men who preyed upon innocent white women. The crusaders revealed that eighty-three women had been lynched in the United States since Ida B. Wells-Barnett had compiled the first comprehensive annual report in 1892.[115]

Although a federal law that specifically banned lynching was never passed, the crusade did raise a general awareness of the horrific practice and roused the nation's conscience to the point that lynching, by the late 1940s, declined significantly.

By the end of the 1920s, political activists had little to show for their efforts. The Sheppard-Towner program was terminated. The ERA was dead, and even many of the reforms the women who had opposed the ERA had sought instead had been defeated or reversed. Black women still could not vote, and activists had not been able to get a law passed to eradicate lynching. White activists had learned, however, that lobbying for causes was not enough; they could see the importance of participating in government by running for elected office themselves. What these activists had done was lay the groundwork for future political activists and their achievements.

Chapter 7:
Women Writers

In the Roaring Twenties, women writers played an important role in the development of modernism, the literary movement that began in Europe in response to the devastation of World War I. Postwar society no longer had confidence in traditional political institutions or in the continuity of traditional patterns of work and family. Old ways seemed to have failed, and in the new age of uncertainty, people went on a sort of uninhibited spree, in literature as in life. The result was modernism, works that jettison traditional literary styles in favor of new techniques such as disrupted narratives and shifting perspectives and voices. Reflecting the modern age, modernist characters live for the moment but search for meaning despite doubt and disillusionment.

Scholars Sandra M. Gilbert and Susan Gubar note that whereas many male writers viewed the modern era with anxiety, "many of their female counterparts experienced the time—to be sure, with important qualifications—as an era of exuberance. One reason for such strik-ingly different reactions was the increase in female power which marked the new culture of the twentieth century."[116]

By "important qualifications," Gilbert and Gubar mean that the Roaring Twenties was not a particularly liberated era for most modernist women writers. After the Nineteenth Amendment guaranteed women suffrage in 1920, many women had high hopes that other barriers to social equality and artistic expression would fall. However, mainstream American society still expected women's literary voice to be traditionally feminine, and hostility toward women suspected of undermining women's home-based roles was still strong. Women writers had little support as the women's rights movement unexpectedly disintegrated and as colleges and professional organizations did little to encourage modernist literary voices, either male or female. The exuberance was genuine, but so was the tension between rebellious writers and the literary establishment.

To support one another in what seemed a transitional time, writers gathered

Vanity Fair was one of three periodicals edited by prominent women writers during the 1920s.

to discuss literary trends and critique each other's works. Historians Carolyn Perry and Mary Louise Weaks explain the value of this collaboration:

> Certainly most artists work in isolation. Perhaps because of this necessary solitude, meaningful relationships with other writers and participation in a literary community can become critically important. The connections may be formal or informal, institutional or personal; they may occur in casual conversations or structured seminars.[117]

Greenwich Village

One of the major gathering places for women writers was Greenwich Village in New York City, which attracted artists of all kinds between World Wars I and II. Caroline F. Ware explains what connected these Greenwich Villagers:

> During these years the Village acted as a magnet which drew to it a wide variety of people with one quality in common, their repudiation of the social standards of the communities in which they had been reared. Here gathered in these years a whole range of individuals who had abandoned their home pattern in protest against its hollowness or its dominance, and had set out to make for themselves individually civilized lives according to their own conceptions.[118]

The bohemian atmosphere of 1920s Greenwich Village suited modernist women writers both personally and professionally. Many adopted the hairstyles and fashions of the flappers and rejected Victorian ideas of femininity, openly smoking and drinking and making no secret of their love affairs. They demanded freedom in their work as well: No longer content to write sweetly about nature and women's domestic roles, they depicted women's thoughts, problems, and experiences (including their own) with unprecedented realism. Some became public figures, both as models of so-called New Woman ideals and as advocates for social and political reform.

The Greenwich Village women modernists were given little recognition by conservative literary journals, but a few progressive New York magazines showcased their work, thanks to the efforts of some influential women literary editors. In particular, between 1925 and 1929, Marianne Moore edited the *Dial;* poet Elinor Wylie was literary editor of *Vanity Fair;* and Irita Van Doren was literary editor of the *Nation* and book reviewer for the *Herald Tribune.*

The women of Greenwich Village proved extraordinarily successful, particularly in getting their poetry published. Some of these poets were commercially successful as well, even though their

Millay's Sensitive Spirit

In an excerpt from his review of Edna St. Vincent Millay's poetry, critic John Hyde Preston praises Millay's keen insight and lyricism. Preston's review is reprinted in *A Library of Literary Criticism: Modern American Literature*, edited by Dorothy Nyren.

A sensitive spirit on a romantic pilgrimage through an over-sophisticated civilization from which most of its romance has been robbed—this is the keynote of her work, as it is the keynote of many other modern poets not so finely tempered or so feverishly alert. . . . Sensitively, and with swift strokes, she has set down, if not the Odyssey of a heart, at least a record of all its poignant moments, its strange terrors, its little absurdities, and much, too, of its mocking emptiness.

Poet Edna St. Vincent Millay celebrated the bohemian lifestyle of Greenwich Village in her work.

works expressed pessimism about the treatment of women and the materialism of American society. Scholars Gilbert and Gubar note, for example, that Elinor Wylie appeared to her contemporaries as "elegantly dressed, brilliantly successful, dominating the literary world with glittering poems and eloquent talk."[119] Yet her poems express pessimism, perhaps best illustrated in "Let No Charitable Hope" (1923), in which she spoke of loneliness and of being at a disadvantage because she was a woman. Yet even in this poem she referred to passing time as offering reason to smile rather than fear.

Even more than Elinor Wylie, Edna St. Vincent Millay typified the 1920s Villager. Already a celebrated poet when she graduated from Vassar in 1917, Millay moved to Greenwich Village and took American popular culture, as well as New York's literary world, by storm. Soon after her arrival, she published a collection of poems titled *A Few Figs from Thistles*. "First Fig," a four-line poem exuberantly comparing her Greenwich Village hedonistic lifestyle to a candle burning at both ends, epitoimized her emotional, direct style. She was unquestionably America's most read and best-loved poet throughout the 1920s. As the voice of rebellious youth— a champion of free love and equality who rejected social and legal constraints in both her writing and her personal life—she was a leader of modernism. But she used tra-ditional, lyrical poetic forms, especially the formal, easy-to-memorize fourteen-line sonnet, so her work also appealed to middlebrow, older readers who liked regular meter and poems that rhymed.

The Algonquin Wits

Whereas the writers who gathered in Greenwich Village reflected bohemian, youth-oriented values, a group of older writers who gathered in midtown New York City projected a very different image of modernism. This gathering place, the Algonquin Hotel, symbolized, according to editor Robert E. Drennan, "urbanity, sophistication, literacy, taste, fashion replacing the old frontier spirit, the call of adventure and the unknown."[120] Playwrights, columnists, novelists, critics, editors, and a few stars from Broadway theaters met for lunch at the round table in the hotel's Rose Room to eat, drink, and, famously, talk. The hallmark of their conversation was wit; Drennan notes that "no subject, however solemn or personal, escaped humorous comment."[121]

Among the mostly male group was a hard-drinking, hard-headed woman, the poet and critic Dorothy Parker. Parker was known for her witty, often sarcastic barbs. For example, she panned a book with the words, "This is not a novel to be tossed aside lightly. It should be thrown with great force." Her criticism was wide-ranging: On hearing that famously impassive former president Calvin Coolidge had died, she quipped, "How can you tell?" And she once reviewed a Broadway actor's performance with, "Runs the gamut of emotions from A to B." She could also be disarmingly critical of her own work: "I was following in the exquisite footsteps of Miss Edna St. Vincent Millay, unhappily in my own horrible sneakers."[122]

Parker was modern not in the sense that she used experimental techniques or dared to explore new themes, but rather because she proved a woman could hold her own in the male preserve of New York publishing and pundits.

The Harlem Renaissance

In segregated American society of the 1920s, there was little mixing of African American and white women authors. Relatively few black women writers were widely known outside Harlem, a section of New York that became a haven for black writers during the 1920s. Yet the decade saw such an outpouring of creative work by African Americans—including a number of women—that it has come to be celebrated as the Harlem Renaissance.

The Harlem Renaissance included women journalists, critics, scholars, editors, novelists, and poets. More than one hundred black women wrote and published during the decade, many determined to portray the real experience and voices of black women. One theme permeates their work: the search for identity. This theme was particularly significant to black women because they had to contend with discrimination both as black and as female. In 1925 essayist Marita Bonner expressed this dilemma in "On Being Young—a Woman—and Colored," an essay that portrays black women's lives as claustrophobic and lacking in freedom. She wrote, "You decide that something is wrong with a world that stifles and chokes; that cuts off and stunts; hedging in, pressing down on eyes, ears and throat."[123]

Harlem Editors, Poets, and Novelists

Yet black women continued to struggle against social constraints. In that struggle they were aided by Jessie Redmon Fauset, an important and versatile writer in Harlem. As editor of the NAACP's publication, the *Crisis*, she gave black women of Harlem and elsewhere an opportunity to publish their works. Many black women poets published in Fauset's *Crisis* wrote idealistic and wishful poems. For example, Georgia Douglas Johnson wrote poems about love and about time and life's stages from youth to death. Another writer whose work appeared in the *Crisis* was Anne Spencer, who lived in Virginia in a home surrounded by a beautiful garden. Spencer's garden figured prominently in her idealistic poems, which explore the natural world and her identity as a black woman. She expressed her positive outlook in the lines "I write about the things I love. But have not civilized articulation for the things I hate. I proudly love being a Negro woman—it's so involved and interesting."[124]

Helene Johnson addressed different themes. She wrote racial protest poems in the language of ordinary blacks, including slang, but she also wrote lyric

Writer Jessie Redmon Fauset, one of several female Harlem novelists, wrote about the struggles of being black in a white-dominated world.

poems about young love. She was one of the first women writers to explore the theme of black pride. For example, in "Sonnet to a Negro in Harlem," her hero is a rural migrant struggling to adapt to city life, and feel a sense of worth.

While many writers and poets celebrated being black, others explored the conflicts that arise when one is faced daily with the hardship that goes along with being black in a white-dominated world. Jessie Redmon Fauset and another Harlem novelist, Nella Larsen, wrote what are called "passing novels," in which light-skinned African Americans pass for white. In Fauset's *Plum Bun* (1928) the heroine, Angela, passes for black or white as needed, in order to get what she wants. One critic noted that Fauset's characters avoid dealing with racial issues by passing: "But when and wherever they [Angela and Anthony, another character who also passes for white] establish a home, the novel seems to assure, it will be one in which the social conventions are observed and in which societal conventions such as racism are not confronted but kept at bay."[125] In her novels *Quicksand* (1928) and *Passing* (1929), Larsen creates characters who do confront the psychological costs of passing. The false identities that her protagonists take on ensure their social survival, but they do not protect them from psychological scarring. As the characters successfully free themselves of the restrictions imposed by race, they lose their sense of personal identity.

Zora Neale Hurston

Like modernist white writers, African American women writers of the 1920s sought to depict uncensored, authentic experience in authentic voices. The most successful, and most prolific, African American woman writer in this effort was Harlem Renaissance writer Zora Neale Hurston. Hurston was trained as an anthropologist. Supported by a grant she received while working on a doctorate at Barnard College, she traveled through the South, recording and compiling black folklore. Initially, she found people reluctant to tell their stories if she told them she was conducting research; then she developed a more creative strategy, which Perry and Weaks describe:

> She bought a jazzy dress, loaded her things into a saucy Chevy coupe, and sped off to the sawmill camps and turpentine woods with a tale about her bootlegging man, trouble with the law, and a need for a safe refuge. Once installed, she would casually prime the pump by telling a "tale" herself, and then sit back and soak up the "lie-swappin'" that would ensue.[126]

This was rich material for Hurston's literary imagination. She also used her early

Zora Neale Hurston was the most prolific and perhaps the best-known female writer of the Harlem Renaissance.

childhood, all-black community of Eatonville, Florida, as a source for her characters, plots, dialect, and settings for her early works. She wrote her most important works after 1930, but she first made her mark as a writer in the 1920s. She had arrived in Harlem in January 1925 with, author Lillie Howard notes, "1.50 in her purse, no job, no friends, but a lot of hope."[127] Unlike northern black women writers who either sidestepped or only hinted at the reality of black life, Hurston treated it with gusto in a full range of experiences from humorous to sordid. During the 1920s she published five stories: "John Redding Goes to Sea" (1923–1924), "Drenched in Light" (1924), "Spunk" (1925), "Muttsy" (1926), and "Sweat" (1926). She also published two plays, *Color Struck* in 1925 and *The First One* in 1926.

With her stories and plays, Hurston helped institute a trend starting in the 1920s to portray the distinctive qualities of black culture—speech, experiences, and emotions—and thus to differentiate authentic black culture from interpretations by white writers mocking or imitating blacks. Two stories serve to illustrate the range of experience, the reach of emotion, and the dialect of the people in her community. In "Drenched in Light," energetic, free-spirited Isis Watts charms a white woman with her Spanish dance. The story signifies the positive side of black experience, the creative spirit and strong, confident self. Hurston portrays the less positive reality of black life in "Sweat," the story of a failed marriage in which a cruel and adulterous husband, Sykes, mistreats his hardworking wife, Delia. Delia does white people's laundry to earn a living and provide funds to buy a house. Sykes hates her independence and takes up with another woman. Critic Lillie P. Howard says,

Though Sykes's vulnerability and uncertainty about his own masculinity are understandable, he is still contemptible. He has not loved, trusted, understood, and appreciated Delia—a man must do these things if he is to survive in the Hurston fictional world—but has instead hated, tricked, and beaten her. As one of the townsmen noted, Sykes had "beat huh 'nough tuh kill three women let 'lone change they looks."[128]

Hurston shows how Sykes brought destruction upon himself with his own character faults. She uses the same idea of bringing on one's own downfall in her first play, *Color Struck*, in which Emmaline undermines her own good fortune because she feels her very dark skin makes her inferior. The theme of the play is the destructive effects of racism and the importance of black pride.

Women Writers of the South

Even as black literary output was experiencing explosive growth, writing by southern white women was in the midst of a boom as well. By the 1920s, new writers had emerged in the South for the first time since the Civil War. During the 1920s there was an outpouring of literature, including many short stories, novels, and poems by women writers.

Glasgow Cuts Nonsense

❧

In a short review summing up Ellen Glasgow's style, Dorothea Lawrence Mann says that Glasgow wastes no words. The review is reprinted in *A Library of Literary Criticism: Modern American Literature*, by Dorothy Nyren.

There is much of Mercutio [a character in Shakespeare's *Romeo and Juliet*] about Miss Glasgow herself. She is gallant and she is a philosopher. She is brave. . . . There is moreover a gaiety, a wit, a joy of living, along with the relentless iron hand in the velvet glove. . . . She possesses a passionate pervasive love of life but she shears away with that sharp rapier of her irony the false traditions, amiable humbugs, even the smaller tricks of behavior and opinion which obscure what is fine and vigorous.

Central to the rebirth of southern writing was the *Reviewer*, a literary journal published in Richmond, Virginia. This periodical published modern works written by both men and women. Carol S. Manning explains the magazine's purpose: "It attracted writers from throughout the South, discovered and encouraged promising new writers, [and] declared war on second-rate literature."[129]

The writers who emerged in the South during this time largely focused on a few common themes. In one way or another, these authors explored how the past affects the present, how the emotional ties to the land affect lives, and how blacks and whites relate to one another. While both men and women explored these themes, women writers focused on social and gender roles and women's character development in the changing South.

Three novelists illustrate how women writers portrayed women characters more fully. One example is novelist Ellen Glasgow, whose *Barren Ground* (1925) tells the story of Dorinda Oakley, who has been seduced and abandoned by her husband and left with their child. She rejects the traditional southern role for women and becomes independent through her own discipline and hard work. She becomes a farmer and gains a sense of identity and strength from her ties to the land. However, only by becoming emotionally hard and cold does she succeed in her difficult life. While Glasgow used common themes of the past and the land, she used them as the backdrop for Dorinda's psychological development.

Throughout the 1920s, the Parisian home of Gertrude Stein (left) and her partner Alice B. Toklas (right) served as a gathering place for expatriate American writers and French artists.

seduced and abandoned through her middle years. Unlike Glasgow's Dorinda, Ellen reacts to abandonment in a traditional, feminine way by becoming soft and sensitive. Eventually, however, she is driven from the land, despite her efforts. Outwardly her life ends in hopeless drudgery, but Roberts's portrayal of Ellen's interior life shows that through close ties to the natural world and by her ability to keep her family together, she feels successful. In this novel, Roberts uses the common themes of the past and the land, but broadens them to explore Ellen's inner spirituality.

A third novelist was Julia Peterkin, whose novel *Scarlet Sister Mary* tells the story of Mary Weeks, a black woman whose husband abandons her. Mary reacts by becoming promiscuous and taking lover after lover. Peterkin describes these experiences in detail previously considered unacceptable in southern writing. Peterkin shows how Mary becomes inde-

Another example is Elizabeth Madox Roberts, who wrote *The Time of Man* in 1926. The novel follows the life of Ellen Chesser, the wife of a lower-class white farmhand, from her youth when she is

pendent by developing the inner strength she needs to withstand the scorn of her community. In this novel, Peterkin uses the themes of race relations and the effects of the past on the present as influences on, but not the ultimate determiners of, Mary's independence and strength.

Expatriates in Paris

Modernists such as Millay and Hurston explored unconventional themes and subjects, but they used conventional literary forms and they lived and worked in the United States. After World War I, however, a number of other intellectuals, artists, and writers, known as "high modernists" because they rejected American traditions and values entirely, went into self-imposed exile in Paris, the center of the international modernist movement. This expatriate community included Ernest Hemingway, F. Scott Fitzgerald, Ezra Pound, and Gertrude Stein, who dubbed these disillusioned writers "the Lost Generation," unmoored geographically and artistically from their past. They produced some of the finest American literature, known for extreme realism, frank language, complex symbolism, and a host of experimental techniques.

No one pushed the limits of language and technique further than Stein, whose apartment and studio at 27 Rue de Fleurus, which she shared with her brother Leo and her partner Alice B. Toklas, became the most famous literary salon of the era. A self-described genius, Stein wrote poetry, plays, novels, short stories, and librettos, and influenced generations of writers in all of these genres. Her style is playful and often humorous, full of repeated phrases and seemingly disconnected sentence fragments. Both beautiful and baffling, her writing has been called the literary equivalent of Pablo Picasso's Cubist paintings of the same era—that is, abstract and seemingly lacking familiar forms.

Though their literary contributions were not immediately recognized, women of letters formed a community in which they could discuss their place in the rapidly changing culture of America and hone their ideas for new works. This community was also a refuge in which they received support from fellow writers. Moreover, periodicals edited by women were available wherever they gathered, offering them opportunities to publish what they wrote. As a result, the women writers of the 1920s truly can be said to embody the qualities of the New Woman.

Notes

Introduction: The New Woman

1. Nancy Woloch, *Women and the American Experience: A Concise History.* New York: McGraw-Hill, 1996, p. 242.
2. Quoted in Dorothy M. Brown, *Setting a Course: American Women in the 1920s.* Boston: Twayne, 1987, p. 245.

Chapter 1: The Defiant Spirit

3. Brown, *Setting a Course*, p. 248.
4. Nancy Woloch, *Women and the American Experience: A Concise History*, 3rd ed. New York: McGraw-Hill, 2000, p. 388.
5. Quoted in Frederick Lewis Allen, *Only Yesterday: An Informal History of the Nineteen-Twenties.* New York: Harper & Brothers, 1951, p. 105.
6. Quoted in Marvin Barrett, *The Jazz Age.* New York: G.P. Putnam's Sons, 1959, p. 44.
7. Barrett, *The Jazz Age*, pp. 40–41.
8. Allen, *Only Yesterday*, p. 106.
9. Beth Millstein and Jeanne Bodin, *We, the American Women: A Documentary History.* New York: Jerome S. Ozer, 1977, p. 205.
10. Quoted in Elizabeth Janeway, ed., *Women: Their Changing Roles.* New York: Arno, 1973, p. 113.
11. Lois W. Banner, *Women in Modern America: A Brief History.* New York: Harcourt Brace Jovanovich, 1974, p. 151.
12. Allen, *Only Yesterday*, p. 90.
13. Allen, *Only Yesterday*, p. 90.
14. Barrett, *The Jazz Age*, p. 47.
15. Quoted in Paul Sann, *The Lawless Decade: A Pictorial History of a Great American Transition: From the World War I Armistice and Prohibition to Repeal and the New Deal.* New York: Crown, 1962, p. 154.
16. Sann, *The Lawless Decade*, p. 138.
17. Barrett, *The Jazz Age*, p. 163.
18. Quoted in Barrett, *The Jazz Age*, p. 168.
19. Allen, *Only Yesterday*, p. 224.
20. Allen, *Only Yesterday*, p. 203.
21. Quoted in Janeway, *Women*, p. 106.

Chapter 2: Coeds and Housewives

22. Woloch, *Women and the American Experience*, 3rd ed., p. 389.

23. Quoted in Janeway, *Women*, p. 107.

24. Quoted in Banner, *Women in Modern America*, p. 151.

25. Nancy F. Cott and Elizabeth H. Pleck, eds., *A Heritage of Her Own: Toward a New Social History of American Women.* New York: Simon & Schuster, 1979, p. 490.

26. Quoted in Sheila M. Rothman, *Woman's Proper Place: A History of Changing Ideals and Practices, 1870 to the Present.* New York: BasicBooks, 1978, pp. 107–108.

27. Woloch, *Women and the American Experience*, 3rd ed., p. 413.

28. Quoted in Angela Howard Zophy, with Frances M. Kavenik, eds., *Handbook of American Women's History.* New York: Garland, 1990, p. 140.

29. Banner, *Women in Modern America*, p. 151.

30. Woloch, *Women and the American Experience*, 3rd ed., p. 415.

31. Woloch, *Women and the American Experience*, 3rd ed., pp. 414–15.

32. Quoted in Rothman, *Woman's Proper Place*, p. 182.

33. Rothman, *Woman's Proper Place*, p. 182.

34. Woloch, *Women and the American Experience*, 3rd ed., p. 408.

35. Quoted in Millstein and Bodin, *We, the American Women*, p. 223.

36. Woloch, *Women and the American Experience*, 3rd. ed., p. 418.

37. Quoted in Blanche Wiesen Cook, ed., *Crystal Eastman on Women and Revolution.* New York: Oxford University Press, 1978, p. 82.

38. Quoted in Cook, *Crystal Eastman on Women and Revolution*, p. 47.

39. Quoted in Rothman, *Woman's Proper Place*, p. 185.

40. Quoted in Rothman, *Woman's Proper Place*, p. 185.

41. Banner, *Women in Modern America*, p. 143.

42. Quoted in Linda K. Kerber and Jane De Hart Mathews, *Women's America: Refocusing the Past.* New York: Oxford University Press, 1982, p. 334.

Chapter 3: Women Performers

43. Quoted in Brown, *Setting a Course*, p. 207.

44. Quoted in Brown, *Setting a Course*, p. 208.

45. Brown, *Setting a Course*, p. 209.

46. Brown, *Setting a Course*, p. 212.

47. Quoted in Brown, *Setting a Course*, p. 213.

48. Quoted in Brown, *Setting a Course*, p. 212.

49. Quoted in Zophy, *Handbook of American Women's History*, p. 236.

50. Quoted in Brown, *Setting a Course*, p. 211.

51. Quoted in Zophy, *Handbook of American Women's History*, p. 172.

52. Quoted in Angela Y. Davis, *Blues Legacies and Black Feminism: "Ma" Rainey, Bessie Smith, and Billie Holiday.* New York: Pantheon, 1998, p. 32.

53. Quoted in Davis, *Blues Legacies and Black Feminism*, p. 24.

54. Quoted in Davis, *Blues Legacies and Black Feminism*, p. 73.

55. John Fordham, *Jazz.* London: Dorling Kindersley, 1993, p. 54.

56. Quoted in Davis, *Blues Legacies and Black Feminism*, p. 53.

57. Quoted in Davis, *Blues Legacies and Black Feminism*, p. 85.

58. Quoted in Davis, *Blues Legacies and Black Feminism*, p. 131.

59. Sann, *The Lawless Decade*, p. 133.

60. Quoted in Banner, *Women in Modern America*, p. 164.

61. Quoted in Brown, *Setting a Course*, p. 214.

62. Brown, *Setting a Course*, p. 219.

Chapter 4: Women in Business and the Professions

63. Barbara J. Harris, *Beyond Her Sphere: Women and the Professions in American History.* Westport, CT: Greenwood, 1978, pp. 140–41.

64. Quoted in Cott and Pleck, *A Heritage of Her Own*, p. 488.

65. Quoted in Rothman, *Woman's Proper Place*, p. 51.

66. Quoted in Harris, *Beyond Her Sphere*, p. 139.

67. Quoted in Cott and Pleck, *A Heritage of Her Own*, p. 481.

68. Woloch, *Women and the American Experience*, p. 161.

69. Quoted in Ruth Barnes Moynihan, Cynthia Russett, and Laurie Crumpacker, eds., *Second to None: A Documentary History of American Women*, vol. 2. Lincoln: University of Nebraska Press, 1993, p. 163.

70. Rothman, *Woman's Proper Place*, p. 50.

71. Quoted in Woloch, *Women and the American Experience*, p. 249.

72. Banner, *Women in Modern America*, p. 156.

73. Banner, *Women in Modern America*, p. 157.

74. Brown, *Setting a Course*, p. 154.

75. Brown, *Setting a Course*, p. 154.

76. Quoted in Janeway, *Women*, p. 128.

77. Quoted in Moynihan, Russett, and Crumpacker, *Second to None*, p. 161.

78. Woloch, *Women and the American Experience*, p. 251.

79. Quoted in Zophy, *Handbook of American Women's History*, p. 328.

80. Quoted in Zophy, *Handbook of American Women's History*, p. 329.

81. Woloch, *Women and the American Experience*, p. 251.

Chapter 5:
Working-Class Women

82. Quoted in Linda K. Kerber and Jane Sherron De Hart, eds., *Women's America: Refocusing the Past*, 6th ed. New York: Oxford University Press, 2004, p. 420.

83. Quoted in Dawn Keetley and John Pettegrew, eds., *Public Women, Public Words: A Documentary History of American Feminism*, vol. 2. Lanham, MD: Rowan & Littlefield, 2002, p. 377.

84. Quoted in Mary Beth Norton and Ruth M. Alexander, eds., *Major Problems in American Women's History: Documents and Essays*, 2nd ed. Lexington, MA: D.C. Heath, 1996, p. 299.

85. Quoted in Norton and Alexander, *Major Problems in American Women's History*, p. 301.

86. Quoted in Moynihan, Russett, and Crumpacker, *Second to None*, pp. 157–58.

87. Quoted in Keetley and Pettegrew, *Public Women, Public Words*, p. 378.

88. Quoted in Kerber and De Hart, *Women's America*, p. 413.

89. Cott and Pleck, *A Heritage of Her Own*, p. 361.

90. Sophonisba P. Breckinridge, *Women in the Twentieth Century: A Study of Their Political, Social, and Economic Activities*. New York: Arno, 1972, p. 157.

91. Breckinridge, *Women in the Twentieth Century*, p. 160.

92. Quoted in Breckinridge, *Women in the Twentieth Century*, p. 160.

93. Susan Householder Van Horn, *Women, Work, and Fertility, 1900–1986*, New York: New York University Press, 1988, p. 64.

94. Brown, *Setting a Course*, p. 85.

Chapter 6: Political Activists

95. Judith Papachristou, *Women Together*. New York: Alfred A. Knopf, 1976, p. 197.

96. Quoted in Rothman, *Woman's Proper Place*, p. 137.

97. Woloch, *Women and the American Experience*, p. 245.

98. Quoted in Woloch, *Women and the American Experience*, p. 242.

99. Woloch, *Women and the American Experience*, p. 243.

100. Papachristou, *Women Together*, p. 204.

101. Quoted in Rothman, *Woman's Proper Place*, pp. 158–59.

102. Quoted in Rothman, *Woman's Proper Place*, p. 159.

103. Quoted in Rothman, *Woman's Proper Place*, p. 159.

104. Quoted in Woloch, *Women and the American Experience*, p. 243.

105. Quoted in Woloch, *Women and the American Experience*, p. 243.

106. Quoted in Rothman, *Woman's Proper Place*, pp. 160–61.

107. Quoted in Keetley and Pettegrew, *Public Women, Public Words*, p. 228.

108. Woloch, *Women and the American Experience*, p. 387.

109. Quoted in Janeway, *Women*, p. 115.

110. Quoted in Janeway, *Women*, p. 115.

111. Quoted in Cook, *Crystal Eastman on Women and Revolution*, p. 117.

112. Quoted in Rothman, *Women's Proper Place*, p. 187.

113. Keetley and Pettegrew, *Public Women, Public Words*, p. 147.

114. Keetley and Pettegrew, *Public Women, Public Words*, p. 230.

115. Quoted in Norton and Alexander, *Major Problems in American Women's History*, p. 351.

Chapter 7: Women Writers

116. Sandra M. Gilbert and Susan Gubar, eds., *The Norton Anthology of Literature by Women: The Tradition in English*. New York: W.W. Norton, 1985, p. 1,215.

117. Carolyn Perry and Mary Louise Weaks, eds., *The History of Southern Women's Literature*. Baton Rouge: Louisiana State University Press, 2002, p. 329.

118. Caroline F. Ware, *Greenwich Village: 1920–1930*. Berkeley and Los Angeles: University of California Press, 1963, p. 235.

119. Gilbert and Gubar, *The Norton Anthology of Literature by Women*, p. 1,407.

120. Robert E. Drennan, ed., *The Algonquin Wits*. New York: Citadel, 1968, p. 12.

121. Drennan, *The Algonquin Wits*, p. 15.

122. Quoted in Drennan, *The Algonquin Wits*, pp. 114, 115, 116, 122, 125.

123. Quoted in Cheryl A. Wall, *Women of the Harlem Renaissance*. Bloomington: Indiana University Press, 1995, p. 4.

124. Quoted in Wall, *Women of the Harlem Renaissance*, p. 18.

125. Quoted in Wall, *Women of the Harlem Renaissance*, p. 78.

126. Perry and Weaks, *The History of Southern Women's Literature*, p. 381.

127. Lillie P. Howard, *Zora Neale Hurston*. Boston: Twayne, 1980, p. 18.

128. Howard, *Zora Neale Hurston*, pp. 67–68.

129. Quoted in Perry and Weaks, *The History of Southern Women's Literature*, p. 248.

For Further Reading

Books

Jules Abels, *In the Time of Silent Cal.* New York: G.P. Putnam's Sons, 1969. A general social history of the 1920s with chapters on cars, movies, popular personalities, and the stock market crash in 1929.

Alan Jenkins, *The Twenties.* New York: Universe, 1974. Discusses styles, sports, cars, airplanes, dancing, crime figures, jazz, and other popular features of the decade. Many pictures and illustrations.

Stuart A. Kallen, ed, *The Roaring Twenties.* San Diego: Greenhaven Press, 2002. This covers unequal society, Prohibition, the good-times atmosphere, fads, and the stock market crash.

Gerald Leinwand, *1927: High Tide of the Twenties.* New York: Four Walls Eight Windows, 2001. Discusses prosperity, crime, race relations, the New Woman, religion, health and education, entertainment, and writers in 1927.

Philip Margulies, ed., *The Roaring Twenties.* San Diego: Greenhaven, 2004. A collection of articles on the consumer society, Prohibition, 1920s culture, anger, and the crash.

Michael E. Parrish, *Anxious Decades: America in Prosperity and Depression.* New York: W.W. Norton, 1992. Part 1 on the 1920s discusses conservative politics, Prohibition, feminism, political reforms, religion, and writers and the Lost Generation.

John Peacock, *Fashion Sourcebook: The 1920s.* London: Thames and Hudson, 1997. Contains 295 illustrations of fashion—day wear, evening wear, sport and leisure wear, and underwear—organized by year.

Geoffrey Perrett, *America in the Twenties: A History.* New York: Simon & Schuster, 1982. This book covers four main topics: the tone of the twenties; the entertainment and fads; bootlegging and crime; and the stock market decline.

Page Smith, *Redeeming the Time: A People's History of the 1920s and the New Deal.* Vol. 8. New York: McGraw-Hill, 1987. Discusses the Puritan influence, intellectuals and workers, the Sacco-Vanzetti case, blacks and the South, and special events of 1927.

Edmund Stillman, Marshall Davidson, and Nancy Kelly, *The American Heritage History of the 20s and 30s.* New York: American Heritage, 1970.

Devotes chapters to small towns, jazz, fads, silent movies, sports, gangs, speakeasies, advertisements, and the New Woman.

Diane Yancey, *Life During the Roaring Twenties*. San Diego: Lucent, 2002. An examination of how Americans lived during the 1920s, including discussions of consumerism, prohibition, gangs, and religion during that decade.

Web Sites

Flapper Culture (http://faculty.pitt state.edu/~knichols/jazzage.html). Describes fashion, music, parental concerns, prohibition, automobiles, and movies of the 1920s.

The Harlem Renaissance (www.nku. edu/~diesmanj/harlem_intro.html). Defines the Harlem Renaissance and identifies its major poets and other artists.

The Internet Guide to Jazz Age Slang (http://home.earthlink.net/ ~klarkins/slang-pg.htm). A list of 1920s slang words and their meanings.

The Jazz Age: Flapper Culture and Style (www.geocities.com/flapper_ culture). Describes the flapper and movie star Louise Brooks, who symbolized the flapper's style. Has links to other articles on flappers and 1920s fashions.

The Roaring Twenties (http://cvip.fres-no.com/~jsh33/roar.html). A list of links to topics related to the 1920s, such as American cultural history, and events of the Roaring Twenties.

Speakeasies (http://alliance.ed.uiuc. edu/cdrom/hononegah/prohibition/ speakeasies-shtml). Gives the history of speakeasies, the risks and benefits of owning one, and an explanation of the crime associated with speakeasies.

Videos and Sound Recordings

Prohibition: Thirteen Years that Changed America. New York: Arcade. Distributed by Little Brown, 1996. Gives a history of the U.S. during prohibition, tells why the Eighteenth Amendment passed, describes the ways of bootleggers and gangsters, and shows the development of jazz.

The Roaring Twenties. Vol. 17. *United States History Video Collection.* Bala Cynwyd, PA: Schlessinger Video Productions, 1996. Explains the desire for normalcy, the automobile culture, the revolution in manners and morals, the rise of advertising, the motion picture industry, and the Harlem Renaissance.

A Walk Through the 20th Century, Episode 17: The Twenties. PBS Video, 1988. Reviews the decade of cars, speakeasies, the Charleston, booming business and industry, and the collapse of the stock market.

Works Consulted

❦

Frederick Lewis Allen, *Only Yesterday: An Informal History of the Nineteen-Twenties.* New York: Harper & Brothers, 1951. A social and political history of the 1920s with emphasis on the spectacles and entertainment of the decade.

Lois W. Banner, *Women in Modern America: A Brief History.* New York: Harcourt Brace Jovanovich, 1974. Presents social, political, feminist, and work history from the 1890s to the 1970s.

Marvin Barrett, *The Jazz Age.* New York: G.P. Putnam's Sons, 1959. A pictorial account of the sensational aspects of the 1920s, from celebrities to flagpole sitters.

Sophonisba P. Breckinridge, *Women in the Twentieth Century: A Study of Their Political, Social, and Economic Activities.* New York: Arno, 1972. A detailed and thorough study, containing much statistical data and analysis.

Dorothy M. Brown, *Setting a Course: American Women in the 1920s.* Boston: Twayne, 1987. Explains changes in women's attitudes concerning work, rights, marriage, and art.

Blanche Wiesen Cook, ed., *Crystal East-man on Women and Revolution.* New York: Oxford University Press, 1978. A collection of Eastman's writings on feminist theory, lifestyles, equality, and politics.

Nancy F. Cott and Elizabeth H. Pleck, eds., *A Heritage of Her Own: Toward a New Social History of American Women.* New York: Simon & Schuster, 1979. A collection of scholarly articles focusing on women's accomplishments rarely reported on before.

Angela Y. Davis, *Blues Legacies and Black Feminism: "Ma" Rainey, Bessie Smith, and Billie Holiday.* New York: Pantheon, 1998. Biographies of each of the women and reprints and analyses of numerous songs.

Robert E. Drennan, ed., *The Algonquin Wits.* New York: Citadel, 1968. Includes a short biography of each of the members of the round table plus a collection of the best quips by each one.

John Fordham, *Jazz.* London: Dorling Kindersley, 1993. A thorough explanation of the jazz movement: the history, the musicians, the techniques of playing, and major jazz recordings.

Sandra M. Gilbert and Susan Gubar,

eds., *The Norton Anthology of Literature by Women: The Tradition in English.* New York: W.W. Norton, 1985. Beginning with literature of the Middle Ages, this extensive collection includes works from English-speaking countries. For each author, there is a short biography and reprints of several short works.

———, eds., *Shakespeare's Sisters: Feminist Essays on Women Poets.* Bloomington: Indiana University Press, 1979. Presented in four parts—poets before 1800, nineteenth-century poets, modernists, and contemporary poets. Each section discusses from three to six poets.

Barbara J. Harris, *Beyond Her Sphere: Women and the Professions in American History.* Westport, CT: Greenwood, 1978. After tracing the source of attitudes toward women as inferior, as domestics, and as rebels, Harris provides a history of how those attitudes affected professional women in America from 1860 to 1975.

Lillie P. Howard, *Zora Neale Hurston.* Boston: Twayne, 1980. A biography of Hurston with emphasis on her fiction and nonfiction works.

Elizabeth Janeway, ed., *Women: Their Changing Roles.* New York: Arno, 1973. A collection of twentieth-century articles from the *New York Times* covering images of women and women's roles in feminism, work, the arts, and education.

Carla Kaplan, ed., *Zora Neale Hurston: A Life in Letters.* New York: Doubleday, 2002. An extensive collection of Hurston's letters to friends and colleagues, organized by decades from the 1920s through the '50s.

Dawn Keetley and John Pettegrew, eds., *Public Women, Public Words: A Documentary History of American Feminism.* Vol. 2. Lanham, MD: Rowan & Littlefield, 2002. Organized into modern feminism and politics beyond suffrage. Each section has four chapters with ten to fifteen documents, each focusing on a theme, such as religion.

Susan Estabrook Kennedy, *If All We Did Was to Weep at Home: A History of White Working-Class Women in America.* Bloomington: Indiana University Press, 1979. A three-part history of working women from 1600 to 1977, explaining attitudes women encountered in the workplace.

Linda K. Kerber and Jane De Hart Mathews, *Women's America: Refocusing the Past.* New York: Oxford University Press, 1982. A collection of articles and documents on American women's economics, politics, and ideology from 1600 to 1980. Also includes appendixes of essential documents, such as the 1920 "Equal Suffrage Amendment."

————, *Women's America: Refocusing the Past.* 6th ed. New York: Oxford University Press, 2004. A collection of articles and documents on American women's issues organized chronologically into four sections. Covers traditional America, industrialization, suffrage, technology, and injustice.

Bettina L. Knapp, *Gertrude Stein.* New York: Continuum, 1990. A lengthy biography followed by chapters focusing on such things as relationships, portraits, language, theater, and novels.

Beth Millstein and Jeanne Bodin, *We, the American Women: A Documentary History.* New York: Jerome S. Ozer, 1977. Each of twelve chapters has an introduction and approximately ten documents regarding women's roles in American history. The chapters include the Revolutionary War, the Civil War, reform, and the two world wars.

Ruth Barnes Moynihan, Cynthia Russett, and Laurie Crumpacker, eds., *Second to None: A Documentary History of American Women.* Vol. 2. Lincoln: University of Nebraska Press, 1993. A collection of published and unpublished essays by women concerning their struggles, work, and achievement.

Mary Beth Norton and Ruth M. Alexander, eds., *Major Problems in American Women's History: Documents and Essays.* 2nd ed. Lexington, MA: D.C. Heath, 1996. Contains long documents and essays regarding problems in women's rights, employment, and identity.

Dorothy Nyren, ed., *A Library of Literary Criticism: Modern American Literature.* 3rd ed. New York: Frederick Unger, 1964. A collection of short critical statements about American writers, both male and female, alphabetized by author.

Judith Papachristou, *Women Together.* New York: Alfred A. Knopf, 1976. A chronological account of feminism, politics, reform, and work from 1870 to the mid-1970s.

Carolyn Perry and Mary Louise Weaks, eds., *The History of Southern Women's Literature.* Baton Rouge: Louisiana State University Press, 2002. An extensive collection of critical articles, organized into four chronological sections. Each explains biographical information, major works, and themes.

Sheila M. Rothman, *Woman's Proper Place: A History of Changing Ideals and Practices, 1870 to the Present.* New York: BasicBooks, 1978. Explains how women's ideals and practices changed in matters of morality, politics, roles, and equality.

Paul Sann, *The Lawless Decade: A Pictorial History of a Great American Transition: From the World War I Armistice and Prohibition to Repeal and the New Deal.* New York: Crown, 1962. A history of crime in the 1920s, including financial crimes, bootlegging, and mafia-type schemes.

William A. Shack, *Harlem in Montmartre: A Paris Jazz Story Between the Great Wars.* Berkeley and Los Angeles: University of California Press, 2001. Explores the careers of American black artists in Paris in the 1920s and 1930s and the reception they received.

Susan Householder Van Horn, *Women, Work, and Fertility, 1900–1986.* New York: New York University Press, 1988. Explains women's roles and work opportunities, often as they relate to sexuality and gender roles.

Cheryl A. Wall, *Women of the Harlem Renaissance.* Bloomington: Indiana University Press, 1995. Includes chapters on Jessie Redmon Fauset, Nella Larsen, and Zora Neale Hurston.

Caroline F. Ware, *Greenwich Village: 1920–1930.* Berkeley and Los Angeles: University of California Press, 1963. A three-part history of New York's Greenwich Village—the community, the people, and the institutions. Appendixes include statistics, maps, and real estate values.

Nancy Woloch, *Women and the American Experience: A Concise History.* New York: McGraw-Hill, 1996. A chronological account of women's political, social, and cultural history from the seventeenth-century frontier to the present.

———, *Women and the American Experience: A Concise History.* 3rd ed. New York: McGraw-Hill, 2000. A more thorough chronological account of women's political, social, and cultural history from 1676 Boston to the present.

Howard Zinn, *A People's History of the United States.* New York: Harper & Row, 1980. A very readable account of American economic, political, and social history, supplemented with abundant quotations that add color and authenticity.

Angela Howard Zophy, with Frances M. Kavenik, eds., *Handbook of American Women's History.* Garland, 1990. Short essays about and historical summaries of organizations, people, events, and themes relating to women's history.

Index

Picture Credits

❧

About the Author

❧

Clarice Swisher was a literature and composition teacher before she became a full-time freelance writer. She is the author or editor of more than thirty books, including *The Ancient Near East*, *Understanding The Scarlet Letter*, and *Women in Victorian England*, published by Lucent Books, and *The History of Nations: England* and *Galileo*, published by Greenhaven Press. She lives in Saint Paul, Minnesota.